The Road MOST TRAVELED

The Road
MOST TRAVELED

by

THE CAMARADERIE COLLECTIVE

Milner Crest Publishing, LLC
Portland, Oregon

ISBN (paperback): 978-0-9820651-5-0
ISBN (hardcover): 978-0-9820651-4-3
ISBN (ePub e-book): 978-0-9820651-3-6

Library of Congress Cataloging-in-Publication data is available.

Cover design by Mako Miyamoto.
Interior design by Jennifer Omner.
Photos taken and used with permission from Scott Toepfer and
Joe Ginsberg. Book description written by Jonah Bayer.

Milner Crest Publishing, LLC
1547 SE 30th Ave
Portland, OR 97214
www.MilnerCrestPublishing.com

This book is dedicated to those who have and continue to live a life on the road, and to our loved ones who've dealt with our absence which is the result of this way of life and work.

These words are also here for the next generation of individuals and comrades, for you who aim to follow the same paths trodden in pursuit of your own peaks and endless possibility.

We wish you all the best of luck in your travels and trust you will find the same glory we've all found, and avoid making the same mistakes that we've all made, in hopes of gaining a better understanding of ourselves and others along the way.

FOREWORD
by Chuck Ragan

Twenty-five years ago, my grandfather asked me if I loved playing the guitar. I replied, "Yea, granddad. I do love it." He followed that by saying, "Well, you're a damn fool if you ever put it down, and don't let anyone tell you any different."

That stuck with me and was a great part of my early inspiration in discovering a passion for playing music. I was raised in the southeast, and my folks were extremely supportive of me—as long as it didn't have anything to do with punk rock, pubs, or reckless living. So naturally, I did what any other rebellious teenager would do: I walked the other way. It took some battling to find my own road, and I found my way into more than one situation, or "home away from home," so to speak, at an early age. In the end, it was all one more crucial page of the book.

What my grandfather didn't tell me before all my running was that following an unconstrained heart and that early passion for music can lead to pitfalls of heartache and lonesomeness with little security, as well as glory, freedom, and pure joy. My parents warned me of all the risks, but at that age I was through listening to anyone. I think it goes without saying that taking an independent stand in life can truly be both a blessing and a curse. If you have a labor of love and want to make a living working at it, you may hit the lucky streak, watch everything fall into place, and land on a big bed of roses . . . or you may be in for a slap of reality. I chose the road at an early age. Although I found amazing places, stories, and people, I've lost just as many. I'll say, looking back on the course of it all, I wouldn't change a thing.

However, despite the joy I have for playing music, despite the camaraderie that I surround myself with on the road, and despite traversing this planet, I do look forward to the end of the trail and taking off these boots.

This book was inspired by a question raised in an interview I did for the

Kalamazoo Gazette. It was actually relayed through the interviewer Jeremy Martin from Travis Dopp of Small Brown Bike: "What is the most important thing that you have learned on the road?" The moment that I was asked this, my head spun in every direction to find an answer. Anyone who's lived a greater part of their life in transit, either for joy or for a livelihood, could easily answer that question a thousand times over.

My name is Chuck Ragan. I'm a singer and songwriter. With the strong help of my dear wife, record label, family, and friends, I've founded the Revival Tour, the independent label Ten Four Records, and have played and toured in the rock and roll band Hot Water Music since the early '90s. I've been honored to play for and invited into communities that have changed my life forever. I've found the love of my life, and she pulled me from a dark place that I never thought I'd recover from. I have built a spirituality, in my own way, within the music that I love. Through it all, I've been a clean, positive, healthy human being, and an uncontrollable, irresponsible, self-destructive mess. Both paths have the ability to build momentum, just as anything else, to become powerful and encompassing in their own way; and whether you believe it or not, we always have a choice about which side of those tracks we run. It's easy to get caught up in the controlled chaos of the road. Time becomes unreal, and the grasp of it can become as far away as our own beds. In the end, it comes down to a single choice of how we decide to treat ourselves, our loved ones, and those who work and live around us.

Travelers who thrive on a path of sensory overload will find an abundant supply of knowledge and wisdom from marvels found and faults defined—as long as they keep their eyes and ears open. Every one of these lives has a story, and every one of those stories has an origin and a reason. And every now and again, someone may be willing to share their story of the joy and tragedy of the road most traveled.

UNITED STATES

EUROPE

KEY

1. Heidi Aho *(Helsinki, Finland)*
2. Paige Anderson *(Grass Valley, CA)*
3. Greg Anntonito *(New Brunswick, NJ)*
4. Tom Barber *(London, England)*
5. Al Barr *(Boston, MA)*
6. David Bason *(New York, NY)*
7. Jonah Bayer *(Brooklyn, NY)*
8. Billy the Kid *(Vancouver, BC)*
9. PJ Bond *(New Brunswick, NJ)*
10. Steve Brown *(Cleveland Heights, OH)*
11. David Lee Burdon *(Sunderland, England)*
12. Eike Bussman *(Muenster, Germany)*
13. Dennis Casey *(Los Angeles, CA)*
14. Lloyd Chambers *(London, England)*
15. Tom Chesire *(Atlanta, GA)*
16. Casey Cress *(Santa Barbara, CA)*
17. Chris Cresswell *(Toronto, Canada)*
18. Pete Curtis *(Bangor, ME)*
19. Tom Dawson *(Portland, OR)*
20. Jake Desrochers *(Sacramento, CA)*
21. Virgil Dickerson *(Denver, CO)*
22. Kyle Divine *(Santa Ana, CA)*
23. Dennis Doherty *(New York, NY)*
24. Ingo Donot *(Ibbenburen, Germany)*
25. Dave Drobach *(Gainesville, FL)*
26. Brian Fallon *(New Brunswick, NJ)*
27. Hollie Fallon *(New Brunswick, NJ)*
28. Kenny Feinstein *(Portland, OR)*
29. Matthew Gere *(Bloomington, IN)*
30. Joe Ginsberg *(Los Angeles, CA)*
31. Joe Gittleman *(Boston, MA)*
32. Xtian Goblyn *(Coca, FL)*
33. Goldy *(Orange County, CA)*
34. JT Haberseat *(Austin, TX)*
35. Sylvia Hahn *(Berlin, Germany)*
36. Brian Hanover *(Sacramento, CA)*
37. Brent Harding *(Orange County, CA)*
38. Kate Hiltz *(Asbury Park, NJ)*
39. Rob Huddleston *(Richmond, VA)*
40. James Islip *(Saltaire, England)*
41. Craig Jenkins *(Santa Barbara, CA)*
42. Juan Kuffner *(New Orleans, LA)*
43. Sergie Loobkoff *(Los Angeles, CA)*
44. Austin Lucas *(Bloomington, IN)*
45. Tim McIlrath *(Chicago, IL)*
46. Nagel *(Berlin, Germany)*
47. Franz Nicolay *(Brooklyn, NY)*
48. Mike Park *(Monte, Sereno, CA)*
49. Nuno Pereira *(New Bedford, MA)*
50. The Rev. Payton *(Brown County, IN)*
51. Michael Semrad *(Chicago, IL)*
52. James Smith *(Oceanside, CA)*
53. Jon Snodgrass *(Fort Collins, CO)*
54. Tobe *(Long Beach, CA)*
55. Scott Toepfer *(Los Angeles, CA)*
56. Mitchell Townsend *(Huntington Beach, CA)*
57. Frank Turner *(London, England)*
58. Tim Vantol *(Amsterdam)*
59. Greg Walker *(From the Road)*
60. Nathan Walker *(Orange County, CA)*
61. Jim Ward *(El Paso, TX)*
62. William Elliott Whitmore *(Montrose, IA)*
63. Jason Yawn *(Washington, DC)*

CONTENTS

Heidi Aho	1
Paige Anderson	3
Greg Anntonito	4
Tom Barber	6
Al Barr	8
David Bason	9
Jonah Bayer	11
Billy the Kid	13
PJ Bond	15
Steve Brown	17
David Lee Burdon	19
Eike Bußmann	21
Dennis Casey	24
Lloyd Chambers	26
Tom Cheshire	28
Casey Cress	30
Chris Cresswell	32
Pete Curtis	34
Tom Dawson	36
Jake Desrochers	38
Virgil Dickerson	41
Kyle Divine	46
Dennis Doherty	49
Ingo Donot	51
Dave Drobach	53
Brian Fallon	55
Hollie Fallon	56
Kenny Feinstein	57
Matthew Gere	59
Joe Ginsberg	61
Joe Gittleman	63

Xtian Goblyn	65
Goldy	68
JT Habersaat	69
Sylvia Hahn	71
Brian Hanover	73
Brent Harding	75
Kate Hiltz	77
Rob Huddleston	78
James Islip	81
Craig Jenkins	85
Juan Kuffner	88
Sergie Loobkoff	90
Austin Lucas	91
Tim McIlrath	93
Nagel	95
Franz Nicolay	98
Mike Park	100
Nuno Pereira	102
The Rev. Peyton	104
Michael Semrad	106
James Smith	108
Jon Snodgrass	110
Tobe	112
Scott Toepfer	114
Mitchell Townsend	116
Frank Turner	118
Tim Vantol	121
Greg Walker	122
Nathan Walker	124
Jim Ward	126
William Elliott Whitmore	128
Jason Yawn	130

Heidi Aho

Full Steam Agency

I'm not a writer and my mother language is not English, but here comes something that I hope can help you . . .

Finland is small country and you need to travel here from overseas, so for many years we had difficulties getting artists here.

It seemed that all interesting artists went to Stockholm, but never came to Helsinki. But things have really changed in the past ten years. We are having more and more artists here—and of course along the way, bigger artists. One of the things is that crowds really love music, like to go shows, and ticket prices are reasonable.

I work every year with over a hundred artists or bands from abroad. Most of the people I meet are really nice and easy to work with. For me, pre-production is the most important job, so that we can have fun on show day. That means one of the main roles is the on-tour manager. Most TMs are super professional, but a bad TM is usually not well prepared and blames everything on local promoters. I make mistakes as well, but I try to teach new people that if you have transportation, a warm meal, hotel, and backline, you're almost a winner.

I started working with the artists in 2001 and have to say business has changed a lot. I think back then artists were more hard and difficult . . . or then it might be that we Tour Managers were just more scared or mad. It was also common that artists had something funny on their riders, like eatable panties or monkey skeletons. And of course, a lot of alcohol. But I think now people in general want to be healthier, so riders mostly include nice foods, nice red wine, etc. It's also that artists can tour for long times, so you can't drink heavy every night—I mean, I would not suggest that.

I think it is also a fact that as the record sales are not very good, artists are more and more dependent on income from touring.

My job is to help artists in any way I can on their stay in Finland. I and our team are always trying to do our best, so I do like to see the same from the artist.

I do understand that artists might be really tired from their flight, and some days I might not even see the artist (except on stage). But I have made really good friends of TMs, artists, or other members of the touring crew. If we are happy, the artist is happy, and we can have great shows and give audiences what they have paid for. At the end of the day, they are the people who make it possible for the rest of us to work in this business.

Paige Anderson

Anderson Family Bluegrass
On the road for 7 years

Well, being in a family band has its own adventures. Life gets a little crazy being around each other 24/7. When we're on the road, Mom (Christy) has learned to pack up and take home-school with us. But it's not always books we've learned from—it's been life as well. Dad (Mark) has also learned to juggle work, music, and all the other stuff that dads do to make life good for their families.

We've heard some great stories, and some sad ones, too. Us kids have learned everyone has a journey through life, from the old to the young. We appreciate everything and everyone around us, and all the love and kindness that has been given to us. It really has taught us all to be humble and to live in the now. Though at times it gets so crazy that we just want to pack it up and say we're done. We realize that with or without the band, we would still have struggles and still have the same issues. We're just leaning to get through them in the public eye, as a family, and stay strong for each other. What a great adventure this has been for our family.

As our papa says, your mind is like a parachute: It does you no good unless it's opened.

Greg Anntonito

LOTS OF SLEEP AND LOTS OF WATER . . . AND COMMUNICATE!

The Bouncing Souls
On the road for over 20 years

Lots of sleep and lots of water. That's my bit of wisdom after touring for almost twenty years with the Bouncing Souls. It's so simple and so obvious, but it's not so easy to stick to a steady diet while touring in a rock band around the world. If you plan on touring for just a week or two here and there, you'll probably be OK with partying and eating whatever—but if you are touring for up to nine months a year, you have to develop endurance and a healthy lifestyle. Especially if you are a lead singer.

I have learned by experience when you sing full-on punk rock for an hour plus every night, you expend A LOT of energy and emotion. Months of extended touring can bring you to a place where you kind of become a zombie with nothing left to give. You find yourself drained, irritable, depressed, and writing songs about busted motels and smelly back stages. Yawn. So if you want to enjoy yourself and put on good shows consistently over the long haul, you have to really take care of yourself and monitor your emotional well being. Communicating with band members is key, so you can all be aware when the exhaustion begins to take its toll. It's important to respect and support each other and remember that you are all in it together, especially when the chips are down and everyone just wants to go home. Long hours of travel and shows can easily make everyone start hating everyone and everything for no apparent reason . . . it's just the exhaustion taking its toll. So keeping an eye on each other can prevent unnecessary band blow ups!

So I guess I have a two-part touring tip: Lots of sleep and lots of water . . . and communicate!

Tom Barber

IT'S BETTER TO HAVE LOVED AND LOST . . .

Backline technician
The Holloways, Frank Turner, the Darkness
On the road 7 years

It's not easy waking up every morning at the crack of dawn in a strange place. Some days you will just wish you were somewhere else with comforts you sorely miss: a television, a shower, your loved ones.

Life on the road really isn't the glitz and glamour lifestyle some would like you to believe. Sure, you can cultivate it into the most rewarding and eye-opening thing you'll ever do, but you have to remember: first and foremost, it's a job. You have a responsibility to provide a memorable experience for thousands of people every night. Once this has been achieved the world is yours, but until you know you can maintain that standard of results every time it is called for, I'm afraid the lifestyle that everyone pines for will have to take a back seat.

This lifestyle can change you for the good if you let it. I left for my first tour as a naïve nineteen year old, but I signed off from the road as a twenty-five-year-old man who couldn't be more proud of what I had done. My friends became my family, my heroes became my peers; out on the road everyone is equal.

Always be open to ideas, be a "yes" person. You never know what could be around the corner, so expect the unexpected. After all, I met the love of my life in the corner of a smoking room, hundreds of miles away from home.

So keep an open mind, be professional, have a can-do attitude, and the road will reward you with the most memorable years of your life.

Al Barr

JUST BE NICE

The Dropkick Murphys

So there I was. I had just got off a plane from Melbourne, Australia, after having been on the road for pretty much three months straight. No record, mind you. In my twenty-nine years of playing in bands, I'd had longer runs! But when it's almost Thanksgiving, and you have been on a plane for fourteen hours and you get told (on the bus to the plane home) that the flight had been cancelled, it's very hard to keep it together. Especially when the next flight is twelve hours later! So I sat there in shock, trying to accept the new deal, watching the crowds of people beat their chests in anger about a situation that the people behind the desks could do nothing about it (except make your shitty day worse!). I watched the last person shake his fist in the air. It stuck with me all these years—it was always in front of me—the answer: Just be nice! I went into that ticket office, looked at those people, and tried to relate by being nice! Wouldn't you know that a short three hours later (not twelve) I was on my way back home! So there you go, boys and girls: You can stomp your feet, you can pull out your hair, but that won't get you too far; eventually that negative energy will get you! What I've learned in all of my years is a lot, but most important, just be nice.

David Bason

I've been on the road on and off since 1995.

I've taken to the road as an athlete, musician, storyteller, industry panelist, as part of a music management team and as an A&R guy for whatever record label I was working with at the time. I've been around the world a couple times, yet it never gets old and always remains the highlight of each year.

Road rule: "Call home every day."

My wife is also in the business, and something we both notice is that when one of us is on the road, even if just for a week or two, there's a weird distance that creeps up on us without our noticing.

It's an awkwardness that takes a few days to get past, when we come out of warp speed and slow back down to real-life pacing. We always get past it, and speaking daily keeps a connection to home that eases the transition and makes it seem like we never really left.

I can be flying across the world to work on shows with tens of thousands of people in attendance, surrounded by major media all day long, in and out of promo sessions or meet-and-greets, encountering hundreds of people in a day—but still only really relate to the people in my immediate circle. My world becomes very small when I'm focused on my team and my tasks. Discussing day-to-day tour workings, issues, problems, or gripes can be easier with a trusted tour manager or crewmember than calling home and having to explain everything from scratch. But there is value in calling home.

Calling home gives you an outside perspective on what you're dealing with in your bubble. It'll take you out of the minutia and get you honest opinions from someone you trust.

You'll also keep the awkwardness at bay when you return because your loved one will be up to speed on what you went through on the road.

Jonah Bayer

BE EXCELLENT TO EACH OTHER

On the road for 11 years

I've experienced the road from many different perspectives, whether that means working in a booth on the Vans Warped Tour, traveling to Europe to write a feature on Jimmy Eat World for *Alternative Press,* or getting in the van to play gigs with my own acts such as the Lovekill and United Nations—and the most valuable lesson that I've learned is simply to "be excellent to each other."

Yes, it sounds cheesy, and I'm probably not the only person to quote *Bill & Ted's Excellent Adventure* in this book, but I think it's important for many reasons; namely because most of the people you'll meet during your journeys have thankless jobs. You might think the soundman in Des Moines is acting surly when he says your stage volume is too loud, and you'll inevitably have to haggle with countless promoters to get your pitiful guarantee, but it's critical to keep in mind that your show wouldn't exist without these people.

Let's face it: It's easier to curl up with headphones and shut yourself off from the outside world—or your band mates—than it is to interact with people you haven't met before, but ultimately those connections are the whole point of being on the road. For example, I met Chuck Ragan back in 2000 because I and a friend snuck backstage at the Warped Tour and ended up running smack dab into Hot Water Music's RV.

Instead of kicking us out or asking to see our laminates, Chuck and the rest of the band pulled out folding chairs for us, asked us our names, and talked to us for nearly an hour. I can't remember exactly what we discussed, but I left that show with a tangible connection and a mild case of dehydration—and here I am twelve years later, honored to be collaborating with Chuck once again on his latest project (although I do wish I could get some of those long-lost brain cells back).

So next time you're settling in on a bus playing *Words with Friends*, try striking up a conversation with a stranger instead and making a real one. My other piece of advice is as someone who has snapped many a Les Paul headstock: Do yourself a favor and invest in an onstage guitar stand.

P.S.: San Dimas high school football does, in fact, rule. Look it up.

Billy the Kid

RULE OF THUMB: "EVERYTHING ALWAYS WORKS OUT. ALWAYS."

Billy the Kid and the Southside Boys
Current Occupation: Going around places/Making up songs
12 years on the road

So, you have decided that you want to go "On Tour." First of all, welcome to the sideshow. We are all friends here, as you will soon realize, and we are (most of us) on the same team. But you will learn all of this eventually, young grasshopper.

Your first impression of "Tour" will likely sound something like: "Wow, what an amazing thing this will be!"

Once you get out on That Road, everything will be so new and exciting that you won't be able to stop smiling. Even things that would otherwise seem terrible (sleeping in a van, sleeping on the floor, sleeping on the floor of a bar, sleeping on the floor of a college newspaper while student writers pull an all-nighter trying to get tomorrow's edition out on time) will somehow become delightful. As you travel those meandering highways and byways, through the same cities streets and truck stops year after year, however, something will change.

We will know that you have changed because we will see it in your Four Weeks Since Laundry Day jean-jacket tuxedo. We will see it in your forgotten haircut. In time, you will become one of us weary road warriors, not really at home when we're at home, and yet strangely at home when we're not.

You will still delight in the simple things. Fresh socks, a home-cooked meal, getting to stay at some kid's mom's house (or . . . gasp! A hotel!?): that real, honest hospitality one can only know as a traveling troubadour. In time, you will cultivate your own precious list.

Gone will be the days of gladly getting paid in beer and beer alone (I know, this seems impossible right now but you have to trust me on this one). Gone will be the days when the van lighting on fire seems hilarious.

But if you can somehow circle back to where you are, right now, as you first set out on this adventure, I promise you will be okay. If you can remember what it was that made you want to do this, you will then and only then become part of a secondary list, a list most in this book will relate to: Lifers.

You will see some friends come and go. You will grow to believe the best people in the world are in music. You will meet people on your first tour that you will know for the rest of your life.

If I could give one piece of advice to any fledgling young whipper-snapper who really wants to get out there on that lonely road, it would be that Fun Is Number One.

After all these years, I can attest that this is still the case.

So the next time you drive ten hours and the venue has been shut down by the Health Department, or some punk kid pays you in dimes from fists covered in tears as he shrieks "I thought there would be more people!", remember: There will always be another show, and everything always works out. Always.

PJ Bond

BE GREAT

*PJ Bond, Butch Walker, the Color Fred, Marigold, Outsmarting Simon—
going backwards*
10 years on the road

Every day that you are on this planet is an opportunity to be and do something great; this is doubly true when you are on the road. Each person you meet will have their own world in which they live, and you will be in it for but a brief moment. For the most part, the world exists almost entirely outside of you. No person is so big that the world literally revolves around them, and to be fair, neither does it do so figuratively.

Do yourself and everyone else a favor and make your impact a positive one. Please do not be remembered for being dismissive, rude, or unkind. Please do be remembered for being polite, interesting, thoughtful, for listening, sharing a story, doing your dishes, cooking a meal, buying a drink.

You will find that many of the fine and talented folks in this book will share this sentiment, and for good reason: These people have done and seen a lot of things, and with that it becomes impossible to ignore the benefits of treating others well. However, this extends to more than just people; it pertains to every aspect of your life. Each time you sit to work on a song, don't just write a song. Write the best song, or at very least, a great song. Don't waste your time watching crap movies, listening to garbage music, eating worthless food. Sure, there are times when you feel you need to eat donuts or engage in the music/movie/what-have-you equivalent, but please, I beg you, do not make this your mainstay. Be honest, be thought-ful, be attentive. Take care of yourself and take care of others. Listen to the people you meet, you will learn from them. Stay positive on the Road, as she has a tendency to feed on the negative, weak-willed, and lazy. Remember your friends at home, and that they don't have to pander to you. There will always be someone willing to tear you down or speak ill, but if you constantly strive to be great to yourself, others, and the world, you will be successful both going up and coming down.

In ten years of traveling in and with groups that have played to any-where from 10 people in a basement to 3,000 in clubs, I can tell you with total certainty that none of this is worth it if you are not happy. Miserable people go everywhere and often stay miserable. Don't get sucked into that. Make yourself great, make the world around you great. When you see bad things, work to fix them, and when you see good ones, celebrate them wholly. If you go about it the right way, you'll figure out how incredible it is and make it yours. I wish you amazing adventures, total love, and com-plete happiness. Have fun, and I hope to see you out there.

Steve Brown

NEVER STOP LEARNING

Yo-Yo Demonstrator
10 years touring

There was a point where we thought we knew it all. We were teenagers, full of piss and vinegar, and throwing bolts of awesome off ourselves every chance we got. And then we learned a lot of hard lessons, the humiliating and painful and not-soon-forgotten kind, and eventually we grew up. We toured, long and hard, across the country and across the world, and everything was shiny and new and we felt like kids again.

Then, at some point, it dulls. You get tired. You feel like you've seen it all and done it all, and you start to take things for granted. You get jaded and weary, and you treat everything like it's old hat.

Seriously . . . don't fucking do that.

I hit a period of burnout for a few years where I just couldn't stand it. I hated throwing yo-yos, I hated performing, I hated touring, I hated all of it. And I missed out on so much, because during that time, I wasn't paying attention to where I was or what I could learn. I wasn't picking up lessons and knowledge from the people around me. I kept my head down, jammed out my shows, and couldn't wait to get back to the hotel at the end of the night. I didn't go out, I didn't see anyone or hang out or expand myself in any way. I was a complete dick, frankly, and it cost me a ton of rad experience.

No matter how tired you are, how broke you are, how little you feel loved or appreciated . . . go check out that county fair. And ask that shy, mousy fourteen-year-old girl at the 4-H tent to show you how to milk a goat. Because HOLY SHIT, IT'S THE WEIRDEST FUCKING THING, EVER!

Go check out the old Spanish fort in St. Augustine, Florida. Stop at those antique malls in Clinton, Tennessee, and look for taxidermy. Those people who are putting you up? Find out if they know how to do something weird and neat that you've never tried, and get them to teach you. Someone in New Zealand wants to take you spear fishing? Say yes. The venue owner also has a pizza place and knows how to toss pizza dough? Deal me in.

Don't let yourself miss out. Don't pass up these opportunities, because you won't know which ones are once-in-a-lifetime until it's too late. So eat the blowfish, throw the knives, climb the rock wall, and learn how to say "Please don't put anything in my butt" in Portuguese.

You'll be glad you did.

David Lee Burdon

IT COSTS YOU NAUGHT TO BE CIVIL

Guitar/Vocals
Former Cell Mates, bass for Leatherface, the Lucas Renney Band, and a
roadie for Golden Virgins
I've been touring since 1999

Tolerance! If you don't have it or can't acquire it—keep off the road. The comrades you're in a band with right now may be your blood brothers, they may well be the best drinkin' partners in the world, and you may have the upmost respect and admiration for the individuals you're about to travel with . . . but believe me, these feelings of high regard will diminish within two weeks of a six-week tour.

Pay attention . . .

The drummer's smelly feet may indeed induce a school-boy giggle on day two, but by day fourteen of a two-month tour, you'll want to saw the fucker's legs off and leave the rotten stumpy imbecile by the side of the road . . . not to mention his breath; where was I when they handed out putrefied seagulls for party snacks?

You may find yourself at a table on day fifteen, sitting between two of your closest allies, eating one of the finest meals that said continent has to offer . . . yet the noise they make when they eat resembles the noise of a German shepherd eating its own vomit from a kitchen floor sprinkled with broken glass, and this can stir feelings of the purest indescribable animosity. Welling up from the testicles, churning with stomach bile, heating up the wrists, then enflaming the knuckles. It gets upsetting.

You will without a doubt find yourself at 3:00 a.m. lurching over your guitar player, clutching that ever-present Leatherman that you used to change your strings earlier in the day, holding the blade to his moonlit throat whilst the odious lump of manure lies there sweating, stinking, and emitting noises that should only be heard in a turn-of-the-century abattoir. The little things seem bigger at night.

The way he sniffs, the manner in which he turns the page of a book—a yawn, a sigh, a catch phrase, the way the idiot holds a pool cue—can make your closest associate seem like the most heinous tormenter in existence.

Just get ready for it, is all I'm sayin'.

Eike Bußmann

A LIFE ON THE ROAD MEANS BREAKING DOWN WALLS

Crew Muff Potter
10 years on the road

There are many ways of life on the road and maybe endless opportunities to create them.

My first period of time on the road was due to job as a warfare material disposal worker. All over Germany I searched and salvaged bombs and grenades from World Wars 1 and 2. This experience created by steel and hate made sure I never forget what happens at the point where communication ends and humans forget about humanity. The point when people believe that erecting walls is better than breaking them down.

The following episode of my life on the road was touring as a merchandiser with the band Muff Potter. Many people in this book can tell a lot more about this life than I can, but anyway, it was a very intensive time for me and I met many wonderful and interesting people on my way. Communication, respect, and understanding seem to be the core, the essence of a life on the road.

Another form of living on the road I experienced is travelling. For my journey through Australia, a friend of my family organized a whole of a lot of things for my trip. He gave me the chance to see and experience things I never dreamed I would.

One day I asked this friend of my family why he did all these things for me, even though he knew I never could give him anything in return. His reply was a story he told me which had happened to him thirty years ago. Way back, his truck broke down when he had been crossing the Sahara Desert. An old man had given him a place to stay until he could continue his trip. He asked the old man the same question I asked him thirty years later. The old man answered, "One day you will be in the situation to get the chance to help someone else." He looked at me and finished his story: "That's how humanity works, right?"

When you leave the main road and beaten tracks and instead follow your own tracks, there will always be people who hate you. They won't hate you because you will have given them a reason. You never will have hurt them or their families, and you never will have tried to take their freedom. But they will hate you because they don't understand what you are doing and they are scared of what they don't understand. But they are nothing compared to the many people helping you and sharing with you.

The road is about leaving those haters behind. The road is about breaking walls down, and not about building them.

"WATCH EVERYTHING,
ABSORB EVERYTHING,
BREATHE IT IN."

Brian Fallon

Dennis Casey

DISASTERS AND MISHAPS

Flogging Molly
15 years on the road

After touring for fifteen years, I've realized that the disasters, mishaps, and horrible gigs are the times and situations we remember the most. They become our story, part of our narrative. They make us better, stronger, and build character.

Like when you've been left behind at a truck stop in a foreign country with no money, no phone, and no idea how to speak the language. When you were playing a solo and decide to do a windmill midway through it and break your thumb, and then have to finish the tour with that broken thumb. When you've had to rip your shirt apart to use as toilet paper. When you accidentally elbow a band mate in the mouth and split his lip wide open. When a bus driver throws the whole band and crew off the bus and you are sitting on the side of the road with all your possessions, in the rain, drinking, playing cards, wondering how to get another bus, and then that bus picks you up and then breaks down and you are waiting again for another bus. All those times your gear doesn't work, the PA goes dead, your monitors don't work. The rain or a fan that wants to stage dive just destroys your favorite pedals. When you wake up on the floor of the van with your face bouncing off the steel leg of a seat.

Those are just a few things that happened to me. We laugh about them now. Anyone who's spent some time on the road has their stories of mis-adventure and calamity to tell.

The fans, and the hour and a half on stage, are what keep us going. It makes it all worth it in the end. So embrace the disasters and mishaps. It's easier said than done, but it'll be worth it.

Lloyd Chambers

BE RESPECTFUL AND GRATEFUL
IN EQUAL MEASURE

Fan/Merchandiser/Tour manager/Tour booker/Promoter/Bassist/
Travelling companion/Fan
First working tour: 21 years ago

In my twentieth year, I ditched my job for a life of uncertainty. The band I went to work for—whom I had been a fan of and travelled Europe to see—brought the ethic of simply getting themselves out to wherever someone would put them on, to get their songs heard back on the U.K. agenda. They paid themselves out of a jar in their shared home. It was never about money . . . it was a gang of friends travelling the country, the continent, and later, the globe, seeing new places, sharing new experiences, meeting new friends. They and many I met in those years remain my closest friends to this day. We shared amazing times with amazing people in an age where there were no mobile phones or internet; every night was a leap of faith. We put our trust in a scrap of paper with a name of someone we had never met and an address we had never visited in a town we had never heard of in a country where we couldn't speak the language.

In the following twenty-one years, I have been involved in most levels of DIY punk rock. I continue to welcome people into my life—and the home of my wife and children—because I have that ingrained love and trust which we collectively share. It is not the internet that has created this web of true global friends; FaceBook and Twitter can't ever make or replace what is lived and shared and what is the reality of living through those journeys and those days. The road is responsible for that unwritten bond. When you have lived and loved it, you will always keep it in your soul and wear it close to your heart, and those you encounter will be aware of that when you meet. It is clear as day.

I am grateful for the opportunity which being on tour has provided me. I am happy that the person that I am, the husband that I am, the father that I am today has been—and continues to be—shaped by my experiences of travelling with friends, seeing new places, meeting new people, and sharing so many amazing and unique times.

Be kind, be thoughtful. Respect the road and be grateful for what it provides and for those who provide this life. It will take care of you if you take care of what those who have passed before have loved and cherished. A band I know once wrote a song titled "Your Wisdom, Our Youth."

Take the baton and run.

Tom Cheshire

WORDS, RANDOM

Writer of poems & songs
10 years on the road

I have been on the road as a writer, entertainer, traveler, and just student of life, taking it all in. One thing I found out is that this world can be beautiful and amazing and we can get whatever we want out of it. It is completely up to us. We are masters of our universe.

Find love then lose it, then find it again. Look for honesty and innocence and beauty. See the ocean from one side to another. Learn as much as there is to learn and never forget it. Your brain is like a sponge. Carry paper and a pen with you wherever you go. Write and document whatever you are experiencing or feeling. If there is no paper around, write on wood, cardboard, or a garbage bag. Sing songs and laugh with strangers. Learn to order a meal and a glass of wine in another language. Hang out with gypsies and dance in the street. Put your feet in the ocean and your nose in the wind. Meet a stranger and write music with him. There is no greater feeling in the world than joining a parade, party, or carnival. When you're looking for a drum, you can use an old suitcase or a bible. Meet old men and talk with them. More importantly, listen to their words of wisdom and let them talk for hours. Play bells and whistles and jazz horns and drums. Have late-night talks and take early-morning walks. When you find someone special, hold on tight and show him or her everything that you've seen and learned.

Take it and run with it, and have the greatest days of your life. Have no regrets; there is time for that later. Live and breathe and love and learn. Life and words and music of pen and tongue, it's a great thing, all of it. Remember, you control your destiny.

Casey Cress

FAMILY

Tour manager

When I took to the road and said goodbye to friends and family, I also said goodbye to the normality and consistency of what some would call "everyday life."

Young and naive when I first began touring, I assumed that life would wait for me, people would wait for me, and I could live this life alongside a normal one. As it turns out, whether I am home or on the other side of the world, life keeps happening and isn't going to wait.

Throughout the years I have spent traveling, more time has been spent gone than home. As a result I have missed many things, such as births, weddings, birthdays, and other events in lives that call for congregation of family and friends.

These gatherings are things that I have had to experience vicariously through phone calls and photos that other people have taken. These are the times that I miss home.

Even harder are the times that I have had to take the punches that life throws, when I'm sleeping on a cold hotel room floor with five other people, instead of being at home with my loved ones. It is these low points that I've found the hardest part about being away. The person you love telling you they can't handle a relationship with someone they never see, while you're sitting in the back of a van. Getting news of a close friend taking their own life, while you're in a smoky backstage room just before going on stage, halfway across the planet. The greatest lesson I've learned on the road is how to deal with these times.

I've tried many ways to cope with the stresses and pains of being gone, of being beaten near to death by the distance. Chain-smoking on the steps of a hotel in the freezing cold, drinking until things stop making sense, taking enough drugs to make sure all feelings have all been destroyed. Although I shouldn't need to say it, I will: These methods are not suggestions. They will not help.

My first-aid kit came in the form of people I had around me: the people I was touring with, the people I spent almost every moment of every day with. They were, and are, my family—not by blood or name, but by the bond formed by all being in the boat together. These are my brothers and sisters that I live with. They are the ones who pull me out of the depths of hurt and depression, and I know they will be there when I need them most. Not bottles of whiskey. Not pills. Not bottling it all up and destroying myself.

So what's my advice? Before throwing yourself off the deep end, look around you and see that even if you're away from home, your family is still all around you.

Let them be there for you and help you up. Rock bottom is a terrible place to be, and worse when you're too drunk to stand up and climb out on your own.

Chris Cresswell

DON'T LET THE WORLD PASS YOU BY

Vocals and guitar for the Flatliners
On the road 7 years

I have been afforded a truly incredible opportunity, one that has allowed me to travel to over twenty different countries on this earth—all because nine years ago my best friends and I decided to write some songs together. When I first began touring at seventeen years old, I knew there was so much of the world to discover. And although that strange feeling of my bedroom seeming to have shrunk has faded over time, the beautiful thing is that, years later, there is still so much of the world left to see.

I was reminiscing with my family recently about my time as a carsick youngster who missed home the moment I would leave the house; for summer camp, or a sleepover with a friend. The irony of what I have decided to do with my life is certainly not lost on me. I am almost constantly in a moving vehicle, and once those tires stop turning I am usually farther away from home than the previous day.

In layman's terms, the lesson I'm attempting to teach here is: Don't be lazy. But furthermore, while you travel, make an effort to experience the different cultures that allow this world of ours to turn. If everyone were the same, if every country, every landscape, and every city block were streamlined mirror images, we would never need to leave home. But the obvious truth here is that there are so many incredible things to see in this world, and it would truly be a waste to squash what we are able to do with our lives and our time into a massively squandered opportunity. Whether you travel all the way to Japan or Australia for a tour, or simply cross the county line to play a single show, don't merely inhabit the backstage room for your entire stay. If you do, chances are your only memories will be of the show you played. They won't consist of experiencing a brand new culture, or seeing things you can't see at home. Aside from maybe some interesting decorations on the walls or a slightly older bottle of whiskey than one normally sees, every bar, every club, every venue is the same in the end. It's what is outside those doors that is left to be discovered.

I continually try my best to harbor the mentality of "I may never make it back here, so let's go make something happen." I am extremely lucky to do what I do with my life, and I love it more than I can express with words. As much as I knew at a young age I wanted to play music, I never thought I would ever see the amazing things and incredible places I have been able to. And if I am lucky enough to return to a city or country far, far from home a second, third, or fourth time, the good news is there will always be something new to discover. Get off the filthy backstage couch and step outside. See the world while you are able to. Not everyone gets to do this, so don't take it for granted. Enjoy yourself and take it all in.

Pete Curtis

THE MOMENT IS THE MOST IMPORTANT

Road Merch
A Global Threat/the Unseen/Heavens/Production manager for Kings
12 years in the bush and 2 in the control tower

During a decade plus of playing guitar for a punk band from empty rooms to juiced-up house parties to packed theatres, sleeping in the beds of strangers' pickup trucks and waking up miles from where I fell asleep to using an empty keg as a pillow and a puddle of beer as a blanket to resting on a comfy Motel 6 hay-stuffed mattress and being woken up by Tom Bodett himself, I would say the biggest piece of advice I could give anyone is to enjoy it all. Soak it up. Grind it out. Eventually hard work will pay off. You will meet rad dudes, dudettes, beautiful women and beautiful men, come up with inside jokes that will bond you to people for life, perhaps get a grip of absurd tattoos, and if you're fortunate you maybe even make some money. Most likely the day will come though, for most, where the fun stops and the slow grind to the grave begins, and if you are lucky enough to have fond memories of a completely carefree time in your life where you didn't have to punch a clock, didn't have to take shit from some asshole boss, and be lucky enough to live in a world where kids lose their shit to songs you wrote, then you, my friend, have indeed lived.

No matter how scary, exhausting, annoying, and unpredictable the road can get, just remember that all the trials, tribulations, friendships, loves, and unforgettable nights will shape the human being you will become as your hair grays or falls out, wrinkles amass, shit starts to sag, and comfort replaces passion. A career in music is indeed a difficult task, and if you can somehow stay involved in it, in any capacity, do it. The passion is contagious, and it is so much more invigorating to work with people who genuinely care about making this a world a fun and better place than having to deal with some schmuck in a box factory.

Tom Dawson

NO PEARL WITHOUT GRIT

The Crash Engine
Portland, Oregon

When you wake up in the back of the van in some vaguely familiar parking lot, you might not remember exactly where you are. You might have flies buzzing around your head, and you might be kinda sweaty. You might still have your shoes on, and you might have a headache. You might spend the next fifteen minutes trying to fall back to sleep, because the sun was coming up when you parked that van; at least you're pretty sure that was the case. But when you finally do get up, it's because you absolutely must find a bathroom, and for that reason you might be glad you still have your shoes on. When it's time to leave that place and push on toward the next show, the van might start making a funny sound. Pay attention to that sound! That sound could cost you a thousand dollars. If it does cost you a thousand dollars, you will very likely be going for a ride in a tow truck. Always ask the tow truck driver to tell you what was the worst accident he or she ever saw. Trust me: Just do it. After you pay too much to have the van fixed, you might find yourself driving across Texas. Don't be alarmed if you make it through that entire Stephen King audio book: Texas is enormous. When you arrive at your gig, you just may realize that you have booked a show at the worst venue in the entire state; perhaps in the nation. When you let all of this sink in, you may start to feel what are known as "emotions." These "emotions" make you want to take action.

Because you have been waiting so long to perform your most beloved art, you may be in a bit of a hurry. You may not see that PA speaker right in front of your face, and you might just slam your forehead right into the corner of it. This could very well lead to a large amount of blood spilling out of your head and all over your face. Your best friend may look at you and say, "Dude, you're bleeding everywhere!" After you reach up to touch your bleeding face, the sight of blood all over your hand could make you start to feel very dizzy, and when the tunnel vision sets in, you might clamor for the door. You may be lying there on the hot asphalt at 1:30 in the morning, asking yourself "What the hell am I doing here?" When your comrades walk over and ask you if you're OK, you might say nothing for what may seem like a very long time. Then you might just walk back in there, stand in front of that audience, take all the feelings you've been storing up, and use them to put on the most skin-crawling, passionate, visceral performance of your life. Then you just might realize what the hell you are doing out there.

Jake Desrochers

WHAT HAPPENS ON THE ROAD STAYS ON THE ROAD

Singer/Guitarist for The Lonely Kings

I know you're probably thinking this excerpt will describe lurid tales of sex, drugs, and all sorts of rock 'n' roll proliferation. However, some experiences stay on the road because they sucked. Plain and simple. There are 24 hours in a day. You are on stage for one hour. That leaves 23 for driving around, broke and hung over, in an overheated passenger van with 4 or 5 other people who all used to be best friends. Band people know this; most common folk or "civilians" think touring in a rock band is non-stop raging and doing lines off strippers' boobs. Maybe it was in the '80s. But late '90s was real. Excess wasn't cool. Neither were guitar leads.

Don't get me wrong. I've seen sunsets in Montana. New York City waking up at sunrise. Late afternoon summer rain in Louisiana that tasted like honey. These sights, sounds, and eye candy are what kept my senses alive out on the long road to rock 'n' roll glory.

If your band got to the bus-stage of its career, touring gets a lot easier but more confined. A van is versatile. It can be a dungeon, sauna, restaurant, dorm, frat house, movie theatre, psychology office, and—my favorite—a night club on wheels. I've always had a hard time turning the switch off once I've begun partying. On nights we drove after a gig, I'd resume my libations en route. I didn't have my license for nine years, and that provided me a wonderful excuse to not be behind the wheel. The van is the fortress you live in as you hurl yourself down the asphalt, living on pipe dreams of commercial success and capacity crowds.

Why it stays on the road. I only tell stories of conquest and sensory overload. I only talk about horrific auto failure and personal meltdowns to other band people. I'd like to leave most people knowing I forged some sort of success or sustainable regional education from travelling in this circus of ego. I've cried, fought, arm wrestled, and gone disco dancing all in the same night, after our worst show. We always partied harder after really good and really bad shows. The bad ones made us party angry, when we drank with the purpose of numbing our senses and trying to find logic or reasons for doing what we were doing. Who wants to admit they may have made a huge mistake by choosing rock as a career? I'd rather fight than die. I'd rather drink than drag myself to the inevitable conclusion that working a real job won't kill me.

If someone were to show me this twenty years ago, I wouldn't believe I wrote it.

Top five worst road experiences:

1. Left rear tire of van consumed in flames. Gas-soaked rag used as gas cap, dangling above. Heat of 110 degrees. Six-mile walk to phone. Tow truck overheats, leaves, comes back four hours later. No water. Gatorade used to extinguish fire.

2. Playing a Croatian anarchist warehouse gig with no running water or electricity. They had a generator. Sign over the entryway read *Burn, amerikkka, burn*. Don't ask an Eastern European anarchist where McDonald's is. They get really bummed on your band.

3. Being chased down a freezing freeway in Wyoming by angry drunken hunters in a giant 4x4, shooting shotguns into the sky to scare the piss out of the California rock band they bumped into at the gas station/bar. Really? Yes. It happened. There are gas stations with adjacent bars in Wyoming.

4. Drinking on an empty stomach. Throwing up in front of everybody as they leave the show where they just paid to see you. The band left me the van in Saratoga, Florida, to pass out, only to wake up with insane diarrhea. Band nowhere to be found. I'm stranded

in a parking lot. It's hot and humid, and I have to hide behind a palm tree to shit and use a palm leaf as toilet paper. I was sweating, cursing, shitting, and quitting my band and all at once.

5. Realizing I left my $2500 Les Paul custom on the front porch of a house party we played in Humboldt County, California. It was still sitting there the next morning, although somebody drew a penis on the case. Fair enough.

There are many, many more stories, but these are just some highlights—or lowlights, I should say. I wouldn't trade any of it for the world. And I'll never feel like a normal person. Thank God.

Living the rock 'n' roll life isn't what it's cracked up to be. It does, however, teach you look at life like a painting, a book, or a movie. What I didn't make in money I made up in experience and friendship. Those are priceless. And hell, yes, I would do it all over again. In a bus.

Virgil Dickerson

20 THINGS TO CONSIDER BEFORE HEADING OUT ON TOUR, FROM A LABEL PERSPECTIVE

I have owned Suburban Home Records for over 16 years; I handle the music marketing at Illegal Pete's; and I am co-founder of the Greater Than Collective. If all these things weren't enough, I book a number of clubs including the Great Divide Brewery, Illegal Pete's, 3 Kings Tavern, and Hi-Dive. I went on my first tour the summer of 1996. While I don't actively tour like I used to, I get out to music festivals and select dates on tour.

Over the past twenty years I've been involved in nearly every aspect of the music industry. I have booked shows since 1995, I have run my own record label (Suburban Home) for over sixteen years, and I've been involved in nearly every aspect of the business side of music. Throughout all of my experiences, I feel like I have put together a pretty solid list of do's and don'ts and things to consider before hitting that unforgiving beast (the road). I hope this will help you get the most out of your next tour. Thanks, Chuck Ragan, for putting together such a useful resource for touring bands.

1. If you are booking your own tour, give yourself at least two months (three is better) to route and start booking a tour.

2. When touring for the first time, start out by doing a weekend or week-long tour, and then eventually book longer tours. Booking a ten-week tour the first time you've ever toured is likely to be more of a disservice to your band.

3. While working with talent buyers at various venues is likely the best approach when booking a tour, always consider reaching out to bands in those respective towns who might be a better in for getting you a show. If promoters and bands don't come through, reach out to fans who might help set up a house show.

4. Just because you have a show booked doesn't mean that there are going to be tons of people there. To make every show count, make sure you have a strong local on the bill, reach out to press/radio, send posters/fliers to the promoter and to record stores, and hit up all of your social networks with the show info.

5. When you confirm a show, get the details of load in, set time, local support, and how pay will be handled. If you don't discuss and agree to the pay in advance, you are much more likely to get screwed.

6. When routing a tour, it's never a bad idea to budget out expenses like gas prices. Average gas price on 9/8/11 is $3.66 per gallon. Use this formula: Number of miles on tour (N) divided by your Vehicle's miles Per Gallon (MPG) times Average Gas Price (AGP) to get a rough budget of gas expenditures. Also factor in things like oil changes, band per diems (if you can afford to do these), and other miscellaneous expenses.

7. Make sure you not only take out a reliable vehicle, but also that someone in your crew knows how to keep the vehicle in proper running order. So many bands have been stranded on tour because the van broke down and the garage needed $3,000 to fix the vehicle.

8. It is very likely that you will have some very long drives. Always have a co-pilot who helps keep an eye on the driver and their ability to stay awake. Obviously coffee and energy drinks help you stay awake, but I recommend sunflower seeds and Slurpees for the times when caffeine stops working.

9. Try to bring an appropriate amount of records and shirts for the tour. You would rather have too many than not have enough for certain shows. Consider this equation: Average number of records/shirts sold per night (A) times Number of dates on tour (N), and do your best to have that many copies on tour. As a label, nothing is more upsetting than when a band says they need records overnighted. Overnight shipping prices are out of control.

10. Even when you do the equation from #9, chances are you will still

need additional records or shirts sent to you. When this does happen, try to give whoever is shipping you the product a week to deliver additional records. Supply an address that you know accepts UPS or FedEx and will have someone there to accept the package. Stay on top of your inventory.

11. While it's nice to be able to stay at hotels on tour, it saves a lot of money to stay with friends and fans. When staying at other people's houses, pick up after yourself. Leaving a house a disaster will not leave a good impression on the person nice enough to host your band. Not only will these nice hosts reconsider putting you up next time, they may reconsider putting up bands at all. When I was in college, I had a band (that won't be named) who stank so bad that their odor was left on our couches even weeks after they left. This was the final straw for my roommates, and I was no longer allowed to house bands. On that same note, shower whenever possible. Sometimes you don't get the opportunity for three or four days, and while you may be OK with your body odor, it might be offensive to others.

12. Make sure the various members of your band each have defined roles on tour. Nothing is more stressful than being the only person handling things on tour. Consider bringing out a roadie to help with the various responsibilities like loading in, running sound, and selling merch. A tour manager is also helpful, if you can afford it.

13. In order to get the most out of every show, make sure you have a great looking merch table, an email sign up list, and considering bringing download cards/promotional items so fans can take something home with them. And while CDs and LPs are great, consider novelty items that someone who already has the record might want. I recommend things like cozies, shot glasses, pint glasses, flasks, stickers, buttons, tote bags . . . the list goes on and you can get as creative as you like.

14. Whether you are playing to five people or five thousand people, you should always play the best possible show you can. Just because five people show up doesn't mean those five people don't deserve to see

an amazing show. And if you put on an amazing show, those five people will tell their friends, and that should help your next show in that town.

15. Having a cooler with food and drinks purchased from a grocery store or Costco will save you lots of money on the road. Example: Buy a case of twenty-four bottled waters for $2.99 total, as opposed to $1.00 per bottle. Stores like Costco are great because you can buy food in bulk that is easy to store in the van. When your band is on a budget, you might not be able to afford eating out every meal.

16. Make sure someone has a smart phone; apps like Google Maps make touring so much easier. A laptop is super handy, too, so you can keep in touch with promoters, fans, and promote your shows throughout your various social networks. Staying in touch with your fans will greatly improve the attendance at your shows.

17. Consider bringing a digital camera on tour. Having the ability to share photos and videos goes a long way. Set up a YouTube channel, post photos on your FaceBook page, and do your best to offer a human element to your blog posts and band updates.

18. If your band is full of boozers, have a plan in place to get on the road safely. Having a system where you alternate sober drivers is not a bad idea. A DUI on tour could be a tour killer. If your band enjoys marijuana, know that while there are states like Colorado that are super lax on carrying the drug, there are just as many states that like to throw the book at people caught with drugs in their possession. There are many ways to safely travel with weed; Google that shit and play it safe.

19. You hear about bands getting all their gear stolen or even worse, their van and trailer stolen. Again, there are lots of safeguards to prevent this. Consider your options, and when parking your vehicle in what might seem like a sketchy place, it's not a bad idea to have a member or two sleep in the van to prevent the possible theft of your things.

20. When your band comes through Colorado, email music@ illegalpetes.com with a head count of how many in your crew, we

will make sure your band gets a free meal at one of the five Illegal Petes in Denver and Boulder.

Thanks for the opportunity to share some of my thoughts. I'm sure I can make a list of fifty tips, but I hope these twenty tips give you good thoughts for planning out your next tour. I think that I will end by saying that not having a label is not an excuse for not touring. If you are waiting to hit the road until a label picks you up, you might never get on the road. While it's a catch-22, most labels are looking for bands that are already in a position to get out on tour and be somewhat self-sufficient. Touring can be really hard, but you will have better stories to tell than your friends back home.

Kyle Divine

Dusty Rhodes and the River Band
6 years on the road

Here is a list of lessons I've learned, in no particular order. Use as many or as few as you see fit.

Things to remember:

1. Wear your seatbelts (or be ready to put them on if you get pulled over). Seatbelt tickets are expensive and easily avoidable. I know that it is not very comfortable to sleep with your seatbelt on. That is fine; if you want to go without, just be ready to buckle it in a moment's notice. Your driver should be ready, in the event that you do get pulled over, to wake everyone. You have plenty of time between seeing the flashing lights and coming to a complete stop to get your seatbelts on.

2. Be respectful to the bands, venues, and promoters you come in contact with. Though there are a lot of touring bands on the road; it can be a pretty small world and word travels fast. I'm not suggesting that you kiss everyone's ass, just be respectful and try not to burn bridges. It makes everyone's lives a little easier and may help you down the road.

3. Try to hit up grocery stores whenever possible. Fast food on the road is abundant and usually the easiest thing to grab while you're traveling. It will suffice, but if you plan on touring for years, fast

food can have a devastating effect on your body. Stocking up on canned foods and some-ready-to eat produce at the grocery store will not only be better for your health in the long run, it'll usually save you quite a bit of money as well.

If you have a morning off and nowhere to go, eggs, tortillas, and veggies can make plenty of breakfast burritos to go around and will usually only cost a few bucks per person.

4. When you're at the point of having a rider, ask for as much as you possibly can. Beer, booze, food, candy, the works. Ninety-nine percent of the time, you won't get half of the items listed on your rider, but in that rare occasion that you get a promoter who has the budget (and has no idea that you NEVER receive your full rider), it's like winning the lottery.

5. When you're on tour with a national band who is traveling in a bus, they're usually getting hotel rooms to shower in during the day and driving to the next destination at night after the show. If you can get in good with the tour manager, you might be able to talk him or her into letting you stay in those empty rooms at night, which can save you big bucks.

Also, some bands might let you clean out their greenroom after they're all packed up and gone. It may seem like you're being a hobo by taking leftovers, but sometimes you can really score. I've found bottles of booze, cases of beer, and unopened bags of chips, all of which will save you money later on.

6. Before tour, make sure your vehicle is up to snuff. Check all tail lights, head lights, trailer lights; you don't want to give law enforcement a reason to pull you over. Make sure your windshield wiper blades are working. You'll undoubtedly encounter some weather, sometime, somewhere, and it is best to be prepared. If you're traveling in the winter months, have snow chains ready. Make sure your drivers are all licensed and legal, and make sure your registration and insurance are up to date.

7. Be aware of suspicious activity. Shady characters all over the world know what a touring band's van looks like, they know what kinds

of valuable treasures we keep in there, and there are people out there interested in stealing it. Secure your trailer, lock your doors, make sure that valuables are not visible to people who may walk by and look in, and take turns sleeping in your van if you have to. On the road our instruments are our bread and butter; losing that stuff can kill an entire trip.

8.   Be ready for anything.

Dennis Doherty

ADAPT TO YOUR SURROUNDINGS; DON'T EXPECT THEM TO ADAPT TO YOU

Hotel manager
Various companies
Current home: New York, NY
On the road 15 years

As a hotel manager for fifteen years, I've had the opportunity to travel the world and live in locations that most would consider themselves fortunate to visit for a week in their lives. I've never lived in one place for more than three years and often spend less than eighteen months in a location. That's a relatively short time to forge the relationships necessary to grow and improve.

The most valuable lesson I've learned in my years is to embrace the culture and differences in the places you may visit in your travels. Having grown up in the northeast, I fit many of the stereotypes: I move fast, talk fast, and have a quick (though not always sharp) wit. This didn't serve me well in Hawaii or post-Katrina New Orleans. Simple things like being caught off-guard when offered a raw shrimp appetizer in Kauai illustrated the differences between an islander and a mainlander. But I recognized I was a guest in the situation, so I took it thankfully and didn't cringe. This small gesture acknowledged an act of kindness from a stranger, and let them know I was grateful for it.

In post-Katrina New Orleans, I worked with a large staff, many of who were living in FEMA trailers and working multiple jobs to rebuild their lives. Having moved there after the storm, I didn't share the experience and was viewed as an outsider. Guess what? They were right. How could I

pretend to imagine what these people had lived through and were endur-
ing to get some semblance of their previous life restored? If I had expected
them to adapt to me, the job would've ended poorly for me and many of
the people I worked with.

Everyone's heard the adage "when in Rome," but it's easy to make the
mistake of expecting people to adapt to you. Simply put, when you're on
the road, that won't happen. If you can't adapt, you'll quickly find yourself
alienated, shunned, or outright asked to leave. Be yourself, but be mindful
of the people and places that surround you. Share your work, believe in
your message, but be conscious of the differences between you and your
supporters. The world will open its arms to you and you'll be amazed how
many places will be better because you were there. Best of all, they will
welcome you back.

Ingo Donot

A MICROPHONE DOESN'T MAKE THE WORDS YOU UTTER ANY MORE VALUABLE—IT JUST MAKES YOUR VOICE A LITTLE LOUDER

The Donots, Solitary Man Records
On the road for 17 years

In the seventeen years of our career as a touring band, running our own indie-label, Solitary Man Records, and being the promoter of various punk rock shows in our hometown of Ibbenbüren, I can definitely say I've seen a bunch of great examples for both nice touring folks and complete, self-centered idiots. An estimated one thousand shows taught me a valuable lesson: Always keep in mind that you are no better than the people coming out to your shows, those who sing or tag along for hours on end for miles and miles, the folks who run the clubs, the crews who help you set up your stuff, the bus drivers guaranteeing a safe travel and a good night's sleep, the friends who are willing to let you crash on their floor . . . basically everybody involved in getting the circus on the road. You are still responsible for your actions on and offstage, and you are just lucky that people like your music enough to support you as much as they can. This doesn't mean you have to take everything and be as modest and humble as possible, but rock-star bullshit is best left out, and mutual respect and support is the key to a long touring career.

I mean, you wouldn't want anybody to pee in your shower at home, would you? Just keep your feet on the ground, hold your head up high, give a helping hand, and savor every single moment with your family on the road! Always remember: The band is the crew is the audience is the band . . .

"IF YOU APPROACH THE
ROAD WITH HUMILITY AND
RESPECT, THEN YOU CAN
HANDLE THE UPS AND
DOWNS."

Jim Ward

Dave Drobach

GOT A PLAN?

Vacationing on tours for 11 years and counting, playing bass with Grabass Charlestons, Nervous Dogs, the Ham, Stressface
Employed as production manager for No Idea Records & Distribution for 14 years and counting

If you can get yourself into a job where you are needed and it's easier for them to hire you back in a month than to train somebody else, you are golden.

Use your gadgets, but don't depend on them. Bands booked tours before cell phones and the internet were prevalent enough to be useful. Your GPS will lie to your face, and if you don't know the basics of how interstates work, you will get lost. Your cell phone will die when you lose your charger. Have an atlas and a paper backup for addresses and phone numbers. These two things take up almost no space and are worth the one time out of a hundred that they save you.

Keep in touch with your crew at home. If you run out of your records, I hope you sold them or traded them for places to stay. (You may have left the entire box behind, or on the roof of your van. It happens.) However you ran out of your new LP/CD /shirts . . . nobody can get you more for your show tonight in San Diego, but they can be sent to you by your show in Missoula, Montana five days from now. If anyone is going to ship you records, give them a heads up and a good address one week in advance.

Don't speed in Waldo! This includes Starke and Lawtey, the tiny towns in between Jacksonville and Gainesville, Florida on Highway 301. This isn't the only stretch of road like it. Share these kinds of tips and learn about others.

It is OK to buy nothing when you stop for gas. That is a hard skill to learn, but it will save you a lot of money. Five people in a van, and each person spends $4 on garbage every time a van pulls into a gas station. Average three stops a day on a thirty-day tour = $1,800 you all spent just on soda and snacks. So why did you come home broke?

Use down time wisely. Read books, learn a new language, write songs. Hours of travel between towns and waiting for things to get started don't have to be wasted.

Say "thank you" whenever anyone hands you anything, for any reason. Stay humble.

Know when to take a break. Take a break from driving when you feel yourself falling asleep at 3:00 a.m.. From drinking, when you can tell its time. From touring in general, when the aggravations start to outweigh the joy. A quick rest will put it all back in perspective and you will be recharged on all fronts.

Brian Fallon

ONE PERCENT

The Gaslight Anthem
7 years on the road

For me, the road and traveling to new places every day was in my bloodstream. It was in the artists, in the songs I grew up listening to; it is what I've been called to do with the work of my hands, so far. The problem I always have is getting caught up in the day-to-day routine. I miss a lot when I'm working. In the last year, I've learned to slow it all down, because I realized one day I'm going to be too old, or too tired, or just called to something else, so I need to enjoy this now. Live today. Watch everything, absorb everything, breathe it in. Nobody gets to do what we do—we're the 1 percent who got to get out. People envy what we do. Let's make sure we live it to the fullest and enjoy every minute of it; we're doing for those who can't. We're writing the story, and we're telling the tales. Make it count. Mean it always.

Hollie Fallon

DON'T KEEP YOUR MOUTH SHUT

Tour manager
The Gaslight Anthem
Years on the road: 6

I have loved my job as a TM. I loved the traveling, amazing experiences, and making life-long friends. I had to get that out first, because in the same breath I will also say that this industry is scary. It can be shady and dangerous, and you can get sucked into a world that you never thought you would be a part of.

I love my boys. I care about nothing more on the road than making sure that they are happy and safe. I'm not necessarily referring to physical safety, as they are grown men and of course can handle themselves; I'm referring to the icky snakes that will slither in unnoticed and try to take a bite.

I ask "inappropriate" questions. I challenge the "authority." I have been told on more than one occasion "stay out of what is none of your business." If you aren't sure about something, or something doesn't seem right to you—even if you just have a funny feeling but have no idea why—ask questions. Talk to your people. Talk to people you can trust. And don't ever keep your mouth shut.

Kenny Feinstein

DO NOT EAT SHIT BURGERS

Touring member and part-founder
The Water Tower Bucket Boys; also toured with Foghorn Stringband
Toured for 4 years

Basically the road can get very tiring and painful. Many times when I finish a long tour, I feel as though I have fought a battle. This is why it is so important to eat as well as you can at all times. Chances are there will not be that many opportunities to eat well, anyway. I always start exercising heavily and eating exceptionally well a week before we go out. The terrible food hits as soon as you get to the airport. So either bring some trail mix and cheese from home, or be prepared to start the decent. Once you arrive to your destination you will probably be hungry, too, so if you can find some fruit—EAT IT. One place that my group spends a lot of time in is the U.K. In the U.K., people take good care of you and want to feed you and feed you and then feed you some more. The thing is that they love to feed you tons of meat. Your body may not be ready for this, if you do not usually eat bacon and sausages five times a day. So you might even think about preparing your body by eating more and more meat before you leave home. If you are a vegetarian or a vegan, you really need to make sure you cover your own food whenever you go to someone's house to stay, because chances are they will cook you a meaty meal. Basically, you need to be properly nourished to be playing shows every night for an extended period of time. Most of the time you will go to sleep around 4:00 a.m. and wake up at 9:00 a.m. to get that radio spot at 11:00 a.m., so with all this in mind, let me put it to you like a road veteran Ivan once told me when I was seventeen: "Make sure you do not eat too many shit burgers."

Matthew Gere

FIND YOUR OWN WAY

Merchandise/Driver/Video projector/Tour manager
Bouncing Souls/Hot Water Music/Chuck Ragan/Tim Barry/the
Revival Tour
5 years of full-time life on the road

The trick in trying to distill years of experience into a single, simple maxim is to deftly winnow the truly meaningful advice from the silly platitudes. The truth is complex and liquid, rules are limber, lithe, serpentine shapes; for all my searching, I've not yet found a simple aphorism that nails down the truth and lays it supine, stretched cleanly across the whole of experience. Surely there are simple lessons that remain virtually true in my traveling experience: Always go the bathroom every time you stop, even if you think you don't have to; learn to live on other people's schedules; stay on top of your vehicle maintenance . . . and harder things: The road is rough on all your relationships; home may be an anchor when you are navigating the uncertainty, or a tide that keeps sweeping away all the things you know and leaves you behind. When traveling, you certainly do learn a lot about yourself and about the world, but they are lessons learned from a distorted, ever-shifting perspective. If your life is based around traveling, then you are a person chasing an ephemeral dream; all things are uncertain and to some degree difficult or strange. You are a dweller of the sometimes-lonely disconnect between all the worlds that inhabit this one. But there are others. Float on and through all things known and unknown, no one thing is more real or important in any one realm than the next, just different. In the best moments, you are creating bright, beautiful destiny from one moment to the next, and you know that you are not alone in the in-between.

When I started touring, it was a lifestyle that I jumped into quite flippantly because I wanted to get away from what I saw as the stagnation of stationary life. I certainly didn't understand the seriousness of it, the dedication that it takes to commit yourself to the road. It is a job, a lifestyle, a way of seeing, a scar upon your interior, a vessel, the journey within the journey. Someone can teach you to play guitar, or fix an amplifier, or drive a bus, or any number of things that you can do to travel for a living, but no one can teach you to travel. If life fills you with wanderlust, than you must follow where it takes you and figure out how to survive. No matter what your lifestyle may be, everyone makes it from day to day in their own way. The journey is not get in, get out, and get on to the next town; the journey is learning how to make it through the day and on to the next, and making all the days connect into something worth being a part of. You are a bullet spiraling through the meat: Leave a heavy mark and then fly straight through the back side. Endless trajectory and all the possibility of another day, as long as you can make it there.

Joe Ginsberg

GO FOR A RUN

8 years on the road
Bass/Guitar for Chuck Ragan, Audra Mae, Revival Tour, Baywood,
Single File

Over the course of my years on the road, one simple rule has kept me sane. I fondly refer to this as my "Go for a Run" system.

Allow me to preface this explanation by saying that when I developed the system, I was what most people would label a *big boy*. At the time I was about 240 pounds, and my band had just signed a major label deal. Shortly after signing, our big shot A&R said to me (in front of the entire band and producer, no less), "You're gonna want to trim up a bit before you start shooting videos, touring, and doing photo shoots. You want to have that rock and roll look, and . . . well, rock stars are thin."

What a sensitive, tactful guy, right? Well, it worked. He definitely instilled the stereotypical LA vanity in me. I started hitting the hotel gym every morning. After every sound check, I would find the will power to run through the neighborhood around the venue and return drenched in a satisfied sweat. At any given spare moment, I could be found pumping out extensive sit-ups and push-ups in the green room. Needless to say . . . I was obsessed. However, my compulsive personality gave way to success, because within a year I had dropped sixty pounds, rendering me unrecognizable to the closest of friends.

Thus my addiction to exercise was set into motion. However, it became increasingly obvious that the "Go for a Run" system was becoming less about losing weight and more about my wavering mental health. Touring for a living is an interesting life, to say the least, causing even the strongest of men to crumble at times. Late nights, early mornings, long drives, terrible food, too much booze, and being away from loved ones for months at a time can take its toll on a person, mentally and physically.

Going for a daily run became my way to shake the tour blues and cope with the life of a gypsy. This is my one rule of the road, and I follow it strictly to this day. No matter whom I am touring with, I meet the day two hours before everyone else, grab my iPod, throw on my running shoes and signature short shorts, and get out of the hotel or bus.

Running has saved my sanity. It helps me to maintain balance by giving me much needed space not always available while traveling with a bunch of dudes. Running provides a dependable constant in a profession that throws you nothing but curve balls. That constant allows me to feel a sense of home whether I am in a place I've toured countless times before, or any city around the world I am visiting for the very first time.

The "Go for a Run" system is the perfect way to

- see the sights
- clear the mind
- shake a bad show
- start the day fresh
- explore new surroundings
- provide much needed alone time
- sweat out last night's bad decisions
- prevent obesity from fast food and late night pizza
- provide an up-close look at natives (rad babes, duh)

I'm not re-inventing the wheel, but the "Go For a Run" system is my jam. Why sit on the bus when you can run alongside white-tailed deer in a meadow, get up close and personal with Lake Zurich, literally lose yourself in the canals and architecture of Amsterdam, or climb through the crisp mountain air of the Rockies?

You can sleep in all you'd like; I'm going for a run . . .

Joe Gittleman

NEVER GET INVOLVED IN ANYTHING YOU ARE TOO DRUNK TO UNDERSTAND

The Mighty Mighty Bosstones, GangGreen
On the road 25 years

In 1993, while on tour in Italy, I was stabbed in the chest by a T-shirt bootlegger after drunkenly inserting myself in a pointless argument over merch turf. It's crazy how quickly a fun summer excursion can turn into a scene from *Apocalypse Now*. As I staggered and fell, my dear friend and guitar player, Nate, shouted, "Man down!" Our entire entourage quickly turned into an angry stick-wielding mob. Eventually my attacker was subdued when he ran full speed into the back of a parked van. As I lay in the bushes, one of my tour mates rushed to my side. "Oh, man, are you OK? Can I get you anything?" I pulled him close and asked him for a vodka tonic. Now, it's one thing to be drunk and bleeding and request an alcoholic beverage. It's another thing entirely to cheerfully fill the order.

After an ambulance ride, some stitches, a couple hours in the hospital, and a bag or two of saline, I was ready to head back to the bus. The doctor wanted me to stay the night, but after some fast-talk and signatures on the release form, I was off. Doc even arranged for me to ride with the police back to the venue. Or at least I thought we were going to the venue . . . In hindsight, the line of paparazzi outside the hospital could have suggested otherwise. Again, I was still too drunk to fully understand the situation.

And now, a few facts to speed the story along:

1. Bootlegging in Italy is an organized crime activity and considered legal with a simple street vending license.

2. During the melee after my stabbing, concert-goers stole the bootlegger's money and merchandise.

3. I was in big trouble.

The mattress in my jail cell looked like a painter's palate of dried bodily fluids. As the reality of my surroundings set in, I prepared myself to do some real time. I pretended the Arabic-looking scrawl on the walls of my cell was advice from a far more hardened criminal. "Keep your shit together, man!" one line said. I took refuge in these imaginary words of wisdom. After what could have been ten seconds of sleep, I woke to a guard banging on the door with a billy club.

Court that day was a relatively suspicious affair. The prosecutor informed me through an interpreter that this type of "crime" carries a sixty-day sentence. I also learned there had been a lot of soccer-related hooligan-type violence in the area recently. The paparazzi lumped me in with this bunch, in the newspapers. After paying a fine of around $3,000, I was on the next train to Rome for the last show of the tour (the busses had rolled the night before, for fear of retaliation from highway snipers.) Our show was ultimately cancelled after my lung started gurgling and x-rays revealed further damage. I flew home and cleared U.S. customs with nothing but a garbage bag full of bloody clothes and x-rays.

Drinking can be a lot of fun, but sometimes it brings very un-fun consequences. Never get involved in anything you are too drunk to understand. It's also OK not to drink at all.

Xtian Goblyn

DON'T GET BITTEN BY THE CONCRETE COBRA

Owner of Rocket City Recording Studio in Cocoa, Florida, and founder of
Bony Orbit Records
Live sound engineer at Hippodrome at 9 Stone in Cocoa, Florida
Current Bands: The Green Goblyn Project (Vox/Gtr) based in Cocoa, FL;
Hydra (Vox/Gtr) based in Los Angeles, CA; H.C.A. (Gtr/B-up Vox) based
in Sarasota, FL; Xtian Goblyn as solo acoustic performer based in Cocoa, FL
Years working the road: Started touring with Green Goblyn Project in 1998;
playing live shows with bands around Florida since 1988.

That's what one of my best friends had said to me years ago, but i never realized the many ways it could be taken. I had been on tour with Hydra for a few weeks because the Goblyn was on a short hiatus, and i decided to follow up the tour with a solo acoustic road trip. It was the last show of the run, and i found myself in Bradenton, Florida, drinking with some old friends. My girlfriend of four years and i had recently split up, and i was hitting the whiskey hard because of it. I let exhaustion and depression get the best of me and took some pills that were offered.

I washed them down with a bottle of whiskey, not caring what the pills were. Before too long i was vomiting and had lost most my coordination. I eventually passed out in my truck, but the next morning i still couldn't stop the now-bloody vomiting. I was embarrassed, so i drove about an hour north and passed out in a wal-mart parking lot for two days, waking up briefly only to vomit the blood that was constantly refilling in my stomach.

When i came back to my senses the slightest bit, my truck was covered with blood, inside and out. I hadn't had food or water in over two days. I bought some water, but I was still extremely sick. With destination: Don't Care, i started driving north again, stopping every hour or so to throw up more. I eventually hit I-10 and headed west. The last thing i remember was slapping myself in the face to stay awake and fight off nausea. I woke up in the bushes off the side of I-10 in Alabama with the truck still running and no recollection of how i got where i was. My truck was in park, so i figured i had just pulled into the brush to rest. I called my good friend in Valdosta, Georgia, and she convinced me to make my way there. I turned the truck around at the next exit, finally able to hold down a little water, and headed east. When i reached Valdosta i was in horrible shape. Covered in blood-vomit and excrement, my friend cleaned me up, fed me soup, and allowed me to sleep for another day.

Waking up from that, we went to get some toast and coffee at waffle house, and she spoke of a coiling river that ran rapid after the rains. It was one of her favorite places to go and think and was only about a quarter-mile hike into the woods off the highway we were near. I agreed that it would be nice, so after breakfast we parked the truck and walked into the forest together to find this secret stream. About halfway there, we came across an old graveyard in the woods with maybe ten or fifteen home-made-looking tombstones. I didn't think too much about that as we passed by.

Upon arrival at the river, it was indeed beautiful! It had been raining a lot. The water was whirl-pooling and winding so much that the sand layers appeared like marble. The late-afternoon sun was peeking through the trees so as to make shadow and light almost monochromatic, and majestic. It was like heaven, and my friend like an angel.

I walked along the bank where there was a five- or six-foot drop cut into the earth by the moving water, taking in multiple perspectives of the glorious vision i beheld, when i saw a dead snake lying in the grass and leaves. It looked like a water moccasin but mangled by nature, pale, with a crushed head. Nonetheless, a large snake. I pointed it out and stepped forward to kick it into the river when it reared into strike position. What i thought was a crushed head was actually a dead leaf that had fallen on its face, giving the illusion of mutilation. With my boot in midair, standing on one leg, i had a moment of eye to eye communication between me and that snake. Not only was i frozen, the snake frozen, and my friend frozen, but the world itself seemed frozen in a time of silence. Then i received a message from mother nature herself. It was "Boy, you better wake the fuck up! You don't even realize how close to death you're walking." It was like a whisper straight to my brain. The snake dropped and dashed off the ledge into the water.

As i backed away slowly, i thought of things like how well balanced i was, when for the last four days i could hardly even walk straight; and how if i had been bitten in my current state of malnourishment, i would have probably not been able to make it back to my truck, and the poor 115-pound girl i was with would have had a hard time dragging me back to my truck then getting me to the nearest place for help. I thought of the graveyard we passed.

I listened to the message i received that day, and i think about it a lot. You can't always trust what you see, or find on the road, and you must always use caution. I understand a bit more what it meant when my friend said, "Don't let the concrete cobra bite you."

Goldy

RESPECT, PATIENCE, PASSION, AND SPACE

Drummer
Yellow Red Sparks
Backed up several times for Chuck Ragan, and backed the Revival Tour in
Las Vegas
15 years experience

One thing I've learned over the years of playing shows and supporting songwriters is you need to understand what your role is as a musician, friend, and guest to venues. Learn how to take your surroundings in before the show. We live for the minutes on stage, but what you will be remembered by is your gratitude for where you are and how you got there. Be patient with your sound engineers and don't be afraid to chat it up with them (at the right time). Most of the time that leads to a more relaxed, better sounding set. Know your role in a band and be passionate about it. Whether you're up front or in the back, always play your heart out and leave your ego at the door. Respect your band mates' space, on and off the stage. They will love you more for it, and it will lead to a longer lasting relationship. Just remember how lucky you are to be doing what you love. Usually the people that last in this crazy world are the ones who have a good head on their shoulders and stay motivated and passionate about what they're doing.

JT Habersaat

Altercation Punk Comedy Tour
On the road 10 years

Touring as a punk-rock comedian is similar in almost every way to touring as a DIY band, save a lack of gear to load around and the fact that everyone you are sharing the van with is essentially a lead singer. I'll leave it up to you to decide whether this is a trade one would willingly make, but suffice to say that the road is certainly not for everyone. Nor should it be. I honestly think the bonding that happens when I meet other "seasoned veterans" of the highways and byways is partially out of an instantly applied respect—you've both been there, are still doing it, and have not fallen prey to the innate Darwinism that a steady diet of cheap alcohol, shady promoters, and occasionally soul-crushing turnouts can reap.

Some things on tour are shockingly reliable. The top honor easily goes to boredom, as multi-hour-long drives battle with afternoon load-ins for supremacy. Coming in a close runner-up is the fact that drunk assholes inhabit every scene in every city in every state, and a punk rocker's sense of humor is generally directly disproportional to how many studs his or her Discharge vest contains. This fact was hammered home upon a recent performance in a quaint, meth-charged town in the hills of Oregon, where my hilarious bunch of standup comic rascals were literally run out of town by a born-again Misfits cover band with a penchant for prison-yard-style violence and heroin.

Still, having toured the country for the better part of the last ten years, I can honestly say that the good far outweighs the bad. The generosity of strangers never fails to impress, and I've done many a tour almost 100 percent relying upon someone in the crowd offering up some floor space to crash on and a shower to decontaminate in, usually in exchange for a few bits of merch and some additional insane drunken road stories. And those road stories can only be garnered through experience *on the road*. I don't care how worldly you are with your hotel and airline vacation excursions; unless you have called the "How are we doing?" phone line on the back of your Burger King receipt in the hopes of winning a free Whopper to make it until the nightly drink tickets are handed out, you, my friend, don't know shit.

Like any other profession, the previously mentioned "road Darwinism" weeds out the crybabies and hacks in short turn, and if you can stick with it long enough (and you don't suck), then life on the road does become easier. Payouts increase to a reasonable level, hospitality becomes more hospitable (heck, you might even get a comped hotel room now and then), and the performer in-fighting generally mellows, as items such as towels and vegetable intake become to less resemble the end of *The Warriors*. And while I wouldn't trade the insane experiences of my rough-and-tumble early touring days for anything in the world, I can say with all punk-rock cred firmly intact that sleeping in a Comfort Inn blows away that time I literally clung to a cat for warmth while freezing my balls off in a heat-deprived barn attic some cocaine-fueled hooligans were kind enough to offer up. But seriously, folks . . .

Sylvia Hahn

MAN ERNTET, WAS MAN SÄT

Booking agent
Destiny Tourbooking, Berlin

Been working there for 13 years with bands such as Strike Anywhere, Descendents, Lagwagon, Pennywise, NOFX, Hot Water Music, Boysetsfire, and many more . . .

I would have never thought I'd become a booking agent. I moved to Berlin and was sharing an apartment with my boss's girlfriend when she told me that they were looking for someone to assist with the day to day office work. That was over thirteen years ago, and something was fascinating, interesting, and fun enough about the job that I grew more and more in to it, and I enjoy it until this day.

The question of what the most valuable lesson is I've learned is hard to answer. There are a few . . .

Some of the most important things, though, are just simple rules most people stick to in everyday life, anyway: Be honest, reasonable, respectful, and friendly.

There is no point in telling the promoter that you expect 500 people at the show when you already know you're dealing with a smaller band that'll be happy to have 150 people to play to.

Put the cards on the table and keep the risk for everyone within manageable boundaries.

You do have a responsibility for both parties—artist and promoters.

I feel that these are basic standards you should follow in life anyway, but it's important to remember them every day and convey them into your work routine.

I also learned about the importance of working well, structured, and thoroughly. Double and triple check everything. You're expected to be dependable, and musicians and crew rely on you so don't let them down. Try to make their life on the road as easy as possible. Try to cover all bases. Sometimes I feel like a paranoid control freak, but as long as it helps not to forget any essential details, I can handle that.

Whenever I have the time and get the chance I try to get a few days on the road. It's always good to see promoters again that you've worked with for a long time, and it's also nice to put a face to new people. I find it crucial for my work to see what actually counts to people while they're on tour for weeks.

Finally, it might be a banal phrase, but "What goes around, comes around" is very true. Treat people with respect and openness, and you'll get the same in return . . . at least most of the time. Taking this to heart, not only do I have a great working relationship with many musicians and promoters, but I can also call some of them my friends.

Brian Hanover

THE CHARACTER LIFE BUILDS

Singer/Songwriter
Union Hearts/Hanover Saints/7 Seconds Road G Revolution Ink Merch.
Owner, Screen Printing and Record Label
16 years and counting on the road

Music was my first love at six years old. At ten, my split-home latch-key lifestyle put me outside, skateboarding and finding others that were living this adventure. Thus I found myself at a record store in 1984 buying Black Flag's "Damaged" and 7 Seconds' "The Crew." I loved what I found out about SST Records and Black Flag and how they toured in their own means. Dischord Records was kids living this incredible lifestyle and community as well.

Fast forward years later: I found myself on the road helping 7 Seconds. Then playing and touring in bands and learning to always find a way to keep that excitement. Not reliving the past, but finding ways to find what keeps you alive, fresh, and youthful as time goes by in a lifestyle that is full of instability, greedy hands, ladder-climbing, and so on. The road is a huge part of what kept it fresh. The new faces, the changing faces, the new towns, or the changing towns. It forces you to adapt, to listen, to understand. Maybe it's me, and I know a lot of others like this. It also can serve as a friendly rebuke that it's not about being on the take, but there is a point to all the long miles, broken down vehicles, often hungry-to-starving stomachs. You are not in this world alone, and the character that is shaping you is also serving as your legacy to others. Does it survive the test of time? Can your family, children, and loved ones feel loved and inspired as well through what you do? Maybe I think too much, but there is a lot of time to do that in a vehicle on land or above. Make your days count. Smile, take a deep breath, and make eye contact with a true heart. People are watching!!!

Brent Harding

JUST OWN IT!

Bassist
Currently with Social Distortion
15 or so years on the road

A list of "practical" rules of the road would be endless. I've been lucky to receive pearls of wisdom from touring veterans, but I still had to drag a hundred-pound suitcase across Europe for six weeks to truly understand the meaning of "pack light." After all these years, I'm still learning small things that I can do to help touring seem more comfortable. One such pearl of wisdom can make some moments really *un*comfortable. It's so simple but really hard to do all the time.

Own up to your mistakes, petty indiscretions, and even bodily functions. No little white lies.

I know it sounds stupid. Everyone knows you should always tell the truth, but we all also know it's easier to skate around it sometimes. Life in a moving metal tube magnifies everything. At home, we don't spend 24/7 with our significant others, roommates, best friends, or family. You get time away from each other to forgive and mostly to forget all of the stupid little white lies you tell. Spending weeks crammed in a van, sharing the seat with a broken amp and boxes of merch with the drummer yapping on their cell phone behind you, leaves no opportunity to forget.

Most of my friends' bands that broke up did so because they just couldn't deal with each other's crap anymore. When I ask them what happened, besides the lack of money, it's usually a list of little petty lies that started the end. So if you fart, own it. If you gave away all the beer to try and get lucky, say so. If you left the van or bus unlocked, admit it. I'm not talking about what you should tell a priest or your psychologist, just the small stuff. All the little things add up. On the positive side, the person that will own all their crap is the kind of person you want in the van with you. You can believe them when they tell you they checked the oil. When they do "the dummy check" at the end of the night, you can trust that they'll pick up the guitar stand you forgot. If the promoter gives them the cash, it's more than likely they are not gonna do something stupid with it. Think about it: If the bass player owns his or her farts, wouldn't you be more inclined to believe them when they say they won't fall asleep at the wheel and kill everybody?

Oh yeah—take naps. Someone has to drive between 3:00 and 7:00 a.m.

Kate Hiltz

YOU CAN NEVER HAVE ENOUGH SOCKS OR ENOUGH FRIENDS

Manager/Tour manager for the Bouncing Souls, President of Chunksaah Records
17 years on the road

The thing i have stressed to myself and to "my boys" is "STRENGTH AND HONOR." it's important to be respectful to and grateful for your fans, your friends, your hosts (promoters, people who work at clubs and venues, people you crash with . . . from the biggest big shot to the guy sweeping up at the end of the night) and to be fun and genuine, yet polite. the greatest thing about returning again and again to a city, or any place, is being entirely welcome . . . to have people stoked to see you and to have a great time again and again. to be remembered as not only an ass-kicking band but as great and honest and hard-working. you only have your word; why not make it a good one and keep it?

Rob Huddleston

R.E.S.P.E.C.T.

Bands: Inquisition, Ann Beretta, solo artist
Touring experience: since 1992

It's a simple concept, really, and one that I found to have the most impact on my entire touring career. It's fairly easy to understate what type of impact your actions can have on your future and from what direction it could then come from. I figure there are a few aspects here that should be pointed out and considered.

1. The fans: This is obvious. The fans are, of course, your greatest asset and should be appreciated as such. You must understand that what you are doing has the ability to affect them in ways that undoubtedly your favorite band has also done to you at some point in your life. Be generous. Be grateful. Be appreciative. Understand that the chance meeting with you can possibly make a difference to not only them but to you. I'll never forget the first time a met a fan (a young girl) who explained to me that a song I had written had gotten her through hard times and kept her from killing herself. It's nothing short of HEAVY. The flipside—I remember meeting a few of my favorite bands, and they were just dicks. Now it could've been that they were having a bad day, or maybe that's just who they are, but I can tell you this: in a few cases, I never bought another of their records and often found myself involved in conversations where I recalled the meetings.

2. The venue, the staff, and the promoters: This one may be less obvious, because everyone who plays in a band has heard some story of somebody famous trashing a hotel or dressing room. Ultimately you have to understand that while you do own the stage for that hour or whatever, it's not your house and you are simply a guest. How you act and how you present yourself to everyone, from the promoter to the staff, the management, the bartender, and the intern that brings the beer to your dressing room, matters and may play a part in your future. I was always very proud of the fact that our agent would always tell me how easy it was to book tours for us and how well received the calls were to the promoter or venues. Nine out of ten times, the calls from our agent were met with a "Sure we'll make it happen for those guys. They're great to have here and totally easy to work with. No problem at all, whatever they want."

3. Your tour mates: We learned some pretty valuable lessons early on from bands like Less Than Jake and All, about how opening bands should be treated. I recall Bill Stevenson from ALL and their tech, Bug, telling me a story about touring with the Replacements, how awful the experience was, and how horribly they were treated. What made the biggest impression on me from the conversation, besides having a little less love for one of my favorite bands (recall what I was saying earlier in item one), was the statement that was made regarding the lesson they learned and passed onto me: "Why do you think we treat you so well? Because we know what it's like to be treated so badly, and we'll never do that to any band we tour with." Point taken, lesson learned. The other lesson there, that we began to learn for ourselves as we started headlining our own tours, was that you never know when today's opener will become tomorrow's headliner.

I recall another conversation during the same tour, where Chris from LTJ says to me, "Of course we're gonna be cool to you guys. If for no other reason than we might end up opening up for you in two years, and karma's a bitch." I can't tell you how many bands that opened for us in small clubs went on to sign to major labels and to headlining huge clubs, selling huge amounts records, and being plastered on covers of magazines. Most of them offered us tours later on, opening for them, because of the way we had taken care of them when they were starting out.

4. Finally, your band mates: This is sometimes easier said than done, but your band is your family, your gang, your brothers and sisters. Everything you experience together shapes not only your possible career but the rest of your life. At times, the touring band family unit may be dysfunctional and the littlest thing (like just the sight of your drummer's face) might bring instant rage, but remember that you're not in it alone. This is one of the few unfortunate side effects of touring nine months out of the year and living in close quarters with the same small group of people. I guess more importantly, just remember that the reason you are where you are at any given time is because of them, and the adventures you are creating with them all started in your basement or your parent's garage.

James Islip

A BEGINNER'S GUIDE TO PUNK-ROCK TOURING IN THE U.K.

Musician and punk rocker, born in Wakefield, U.K. and currently residing in Saltaire, West Yorkshire. Served time in various bands most notably That Fucking Tank and The Magnificent. Recently started touring as a solo artist.
My first tour was Scandinavia in 2001 and I have travelled as a musician ever since.

Thanks to up-to-the-second research methods and severe use of the M1, I have put together a guide that will hopefully highlight some of the pitfalls and tribulations you may find in our humble isle.

"Money"

The most common way these days to get gigs is on the internet. Difficulties arise because of the anonymity people can have via email contact. It can be impossible to tell whether or not the "promoter" you have met online is a cool guy or a ruthless bull-shitter hell-bent on ruining your life.

It won't take you long to work out which category s/he will fall into. Things will seem positive if you are greeted warmly, with ales and a hot meal. If however the promoter offers you the sandwich s/he made for you six weeks ago and asks if you want to trade some pills for your Telecaster, you're probably leaving empty-pocketed.

Before accepting any gig, make sure you ask the promoter if he will "cover the band's costs." This is code that the promoter will interpret as NOT GIVING YOU ANY MONEY AT ALL. Instead of cash, s/he will provide you with a tearful story about just being made redundant, or how they had to trade a vital organ just to use the photocopier in Office World.

"Sleep"

High intensity musical performance and liver-destroying drinking antics can make aspiring mega-punks very sleepy. Usually, it is best to try and stay the night with friends (or even at your own house, if you have one) and thus avoid gambling on the promoter's domestic situation. If s/he is aged between fourteen and seventeen, chances are you'll be sleeping in Mum's bed (with Dad). They might live in a cave, squat, or boat. You may get presented with a bed made of broken glass, fag-ends, and moldy sheets.

Worse still, you could be taken by the promoter to a third-party's abode, thus forcing you to inflict your crusty lifestyle on the promoter's unsuspecting partner/friend. The drug-addled promoter chews his mouth off all night, forcing you to stay up with him, drinking and talking about "the scene."

To be certain of avoiding socially challenging situations, you should always sleep in your car/van. Even in winter, with a hand brake pressing up your arse, you'll find it preferable to most of the above.

"Food"

Some promoters think that many musicians don't eat and simply fuel themselves on pints of booze all night. Worse still, most U.K. cities are trying to cull population figures by only offering unhealthy/repulsive meals to citizens, usually in the guise of the Subway sandwich. This particular outlet is, unfortunately, the only eatery open to the musician post-6:00 p.m. Prepare yourself by going to shops in the daytime and buying fruit—a great vitamin provider.

You probably won't start out with any money, but you don't let that stop you. You only have to pay for musical equipment, vans/fuel/insurance . . . not to mention the money invested in releasing your debut album on triple-minidisc. You can soon get on the road and start earning!

You can stockpile food in your tour vehicle for use later. (Food stocks usually decay and turn into compost, which you can sell to gardeners to help balance the books post-tour.)

Try and tell the promoter in advance of any dietary requirements you may have.

You may have particular meals you like, brands of beer that you prefer, or canapés on the stage when you perform. There is no harm in being as particular as you like; you won't end up with any of it, anyway.

"Navigation"

It is traditional to arrange the places you plan to play in an order that will maximize the amount of miles to travel. This means you can avoid spending endless, pointless hours on the motorway, thus instilling "cabin fever" within yours and the minds of your companions.

Fatigue and insanity can be used to enhance a musician's image; tiredness can make you look bohemian and therefore cool. Not washing your hair, clothes, and skin can help this, too. You know you've gone too far when your own mother says something like "Are you looking after yourself?"

"Future"

From the 1920s onward, it was necessary to have a band and/or songs in order for you to perform to people and hence "go on tour." Nowadays you can use a social networking page to create the illusion of having a band/songs without having to waste any creative energy. Using pre-defined categories, such as photos, influences, etc., you can pretty much say everything you need to, artistically speaking, about your band/music. Playing gigs online, from the comfort of your own bedroom, will become commonplace within the next few years, making the traveling, eating, and sleeping parts of touring much less hassle.

Enjoy yourself and stay safe.

"MUSIC IS THE BUSINESS
OF LIFE AND ALL THE
CURVEBALLS SHE CHUCKS
AT YOU. THE GRACE IN
WHICH YOU FIELD THEM
AND THE WAY YOU TREAT
THOSE AROUND YOU IN
THE PROCESS WILL DICTATE
YOUR SUCCESS AND
SURVIVAL."

Craig Jenkins

Craig Jenkins

I WAS ORIGINALLY GOING TO TITLE THIS "DON'T EAT TRUCK STOP SUSHI," BUT SETTLED FOR "IT'S THE LITTLE THINGS"

Owner/Operator of Velvet Jones Live Music Venue, 2000–present
Tour manager/Sound engineer for Abloom
Bus driver for Frank Turner, Black Pacific
Shared the road with Social Distortion, Lucero, Rise Against, Flogging Molly, Against Me!
Off and on the road for 7 years

In the last eleven years of owning and operating a small live music venue, I have had the privilege of booking/working with bands at all the various stages of their careers. Some on the way up, some on the way down, and some at their highest level of success. As you can imagine, certain attributes of behavior are consistent with artists that are able to achieve longevity in this business. Individually these might not seem like much, but collectively they deserve the utmost respect.

I'm always impressed when I see bands at the top of their game take a genuine interest in the up-and-coming artists that are opening for them. This tiny gesture of standing side-stage while artists on the rise play their hearts out to impress them speaks volumes to the seasoned veteran's character and obvious love for music. On even rarer occasions, having the headliner invite an opening band member or two to share the stage and add their talents to an old favorite truly sets the bar high in my book. This showcases a very unique ability to inspire and be inspired, which is becoming more and more of a rarity in this world. It also conveys the idea that if you were to take money out of the equation, music isn't meant to be mine or yours but is rather to be shared, respected, enjoyed, and sung by the masses. (How hippie of me.)

I've never been a touring musician but rather always behind the scenes. I think the underlying theme of this passage is *appreciation* (AND: Don't be an asshole). I've been fortunate enough to surround myself with artists that never talk down to or disrespect the people that are making their shows possible (unless, of course, we fuck up). Artists that take the time to introduce themselves to the crew (even when everyone on earth knows who they are), or even dish out compliments on a job well done, shows an undeniable sense of humility and displays a huge message of respect for the process. I'll never forget earlier this year (January 2011), when the Foo Fighters decided to do a secret show at my club and Dave Grohl walked up to me, put his hand out and said, "Hey, how's it going? My name's Dave." He then proceeded to thank me for letting them have their show at my club. I was blown away that someone at that point in their career could be so humble and grateful to play at a club that was hardly big enough for their guest list.

John C from Lucero once told me, "We make it rock and you make it roll," (referring to the behind-the-scenes crew). It's these little exchanges that make you feel like an integral piece of the puzzle. One thing that I've noticed is that the higher up the musical food chain you go, the more of these types of people you will encounter. The machine tends to chew up and spit out the ones that can't see the big picture pretty early on (at least, I'd like to think so).

Over the years, I've personally witnessed artists reach success with one band and then decide to start over in a completely different direction ten to twenty years later (successfully, I might add). I've seen the drinking become less about getting laid and more about drowning the demons and just being able to fall asleep. I've watched the money and success of various artists come and go, and come again, sometimes coinciding with stints in rehab. Music is the business of life and all the curveballs she chucks at you. The grace in which you field them and the way you treat those around you in the process will dictate your success and survival.

As I grow older in this business, it becomes less about the money and more about the shared experiences and relationships developed. Five years from now, I'm not going to remember how much money I made or spent in England this year for the Reading and Leeds festivals. What will stand out is being asked by Frank Turner to play harmonica with him in front of 50,000 people. As if that wasn't enough, shaking hands with Chuck Ragan as he offered up a very sincere "Great job" moments later as I exited the stage was the icing on the cake. I can't put a price on being able to live in their worlds, if even only for a few measures. It's these stories that I will now be able to pass on to future generations of musicians and music lovers alike that clearly illustrate the kind of people the younger generation should be looking up to as role models.

After reading this again and again in my hotel room in Clifton Park, New York, while waiting to drive a band to Toronto, I can't help but be reminded by something my late grandma Rose always told me: "It's nice to be important, but it's more important to be nice." As juvenile and "after-school special" as that sounds, it couldn't be more true.

P.S.: Seriously, don't eat truck-stop sushi.

Juan Kuffner

EXPLORE THE REMOTE CORNERS OF THE WORLD

Songwriter, Singer, Accordionist
Band manager: The Zydepunks
Traveling and touring since 1994

I see a lot of bands go through the motions when they're on the road, checking in, playing, checking out, sleeping, moving on. And to me this defeats the reason you should get out on the road in the first place. You're not just going from place to place; you are creating an opportunity to explore and meet real people in a way you would have a much harder time doing if you were just traveling there without your music backing you up.

I'm always stunned by the lack of interest I see in other musicians, and even friends, when I'm traveling. To me, it's an opportunity. I've always loved playing in some of the more remote places in the world, whether it's a Belgian prison or a commune in Virginia or a Texas oil town. You learn more from being in isolated parts of the world where most people wouldn't dream of going on vacation. You meet people who get no support from media, who are surrounded by cover-bands and commercial radio but still have independent bands, theaters, and art spaces—all off the sweat of their own collective backs.

Even in the most depressing places on earth I've found people incredibly interesting, if you just stop and hear their voices. They're out there trying to listen to you and appreciate what you're doing. I've heard other musicians bitch about "rednecks" or "people who don't speak English," and all kinds of other bullshit. If they're coming to see you, maybe it's because you're bringing something to the table that they are interested in and can learn from. And maybe you can even learn something from them.

Keep an open mind. Even in the most God-forsaken parts of the world, you will find good people doing good things. In fact, you're even more likely to find amazing things there.

Sergie Loobkoff

OLD-MAN TOURING ADVICE

Guitarist
Such no-name acts as Samiam, Knapsack, and Solea
On the road 21 years

There are so many mistakes to be made, I could write my own book on this. Yeah, you have to bring a lot of socks yet pack as light as you can . . . Your ex-Foghat-roadie-uncle can fill you in on the specifics of that.

This is kinda mundane, but I think the most important thing I've learned is to lower expectations. I don't mean your expectation of how big shows will be or how well you are received . . . although that is super helpful. I mean your expectations of other people, particularly your band mates.

If you haven't toured before, I'll tell you: There is always going to be one guy that always crawls onto the loft first. The guy that hides during load-ins or will be absentmindedly eating a cheese sandwich at 3:00 a.m., watching you and the drummer going back and forth from the club to van, loading heavy stuff. He is also probably going to be the guy that never helps sell merch but will walk up to the booth during the show and block the table because he's bored. He never drives, either. I used to get so furious at stuff like this.

But as soon as you let that shit go and don't expect them to act differently, it doesn't bother you as much. You can't change your band mates; once you realize that, you're golden.

I do sound like "Grandpa Serg"? Do I redeem myself if I change my answer to "Bring lots of condoms"?

Austin Lucas

RELAX (OR BECOME A ZEN MASTER)

I've lived through many assorted and potentially negative situations in my fourteen years as a touring musician. Situations that have ranged all the way from the life threatening to the mind-numbingly boring. Through it all, I've found that the best thing a person can do is simply this: Relax, and don't let your anxiety (or boredom) get the better of you.

In 2003, I packed up all my clothes, my amp, and my instruments, and moved to the Czech Republic. Initially, the idea was to help my brother with his fledgling bar, although I carried with me the obvious musical aspirations and desires. After making a few rudimentary contacts in the Prague music scene, I was convinced by my friend, Bourek, that I should start by playing as many odd and out-of-the-way towns and cities as I could. The first couple of years, he booked me gigs all over the Czech Republic, billing me as the token American "Country guy." I left—almost literally—not a corner of that country unvisited. At the time, I spoke only a few words of the Czech language. Nearly every weekend, they had me traveling alone, by bus, and to areas where little to no English was spoken. As someone who has spent any amount of time in bus stations (in any country) can tell you, the most interesting sort of folks are always in abundance. Drug dealers, pick pockets, prostitutes, the criminally or hilariously insane, and, in central/eastern Europe, Nazi football hooligans.

As an anarcho punk and a foreigner, I was, for all intents and purposes, the worst combination a human person can be in the eyes of said hooligans. Being alone makes you easy pickings, and being frightened only worsens things. Yet if there is one thing that I've learned about being in any potentially hostile environment, it is that panic is your worst enemy. People generally tend to prey on the weak and scared much more often than the confident and collected.

No matter how frightening or shady an area or situation is, be confident. Stand up for yourself and, above all, stay calm.

The same can go for any person who finds themselves stuck in a high-stress situation. Whether it be gridlocked traffic or getting stranded due to a situation with a broken-down vehicle, the only thing that can make any of these variables worse is allowing oneself to become aggravated. Remember, you are the master or mistress of your destiny. You may not be able to control everything that happens to you, but you can control the way in which you allow it to affect you and the others around you. Therefore, when you find yourself in a situation where the immediate conclusion is that nothing worse can happen, remember that the way you react under pressure can directly affect the outcome, be it positively or negatively. As I said before, RELAX. Your band mates, your traveling companions, and your blood pressure, will thank you.

Tim McIlrath

DON'T TOUR HARDER; TOUR SMARTER

Rise Against
11 years of full-time touring

I never set out to be a touring musician, I'll be honest. I had sort of a hyper-realistic view of how my life might unfold and didn't think playing music for a living would have ever factored into that view. I simply just didn't see it as a possibility. So when our band snowballed and turned into something that I could do as more than just playing around for fun, I found myself facing many elements of the playing music/touring world I never thought about before. But above all, I don't complain about what I do. My problems are high class, and I'm lucky to have such problems. Tour is a grind, but it's a grind we choose, and many would trade places with me in a second. The lesson I've learned from all of it is: Don't tour harder, tour smarter. My band mates and I have families and friends back home that we value and who have often gone neglected in our younger, more suicidal, touring days. Nowadays we look at our endeavors as a marathon, not a sprint. We are lifers. We've committed. We are locals who have been around long enough to see the tourists come and go year after year, but we are here to stay. We've watched the mistakes made. I've seen bands chase success so rabidly that they implode disastrously. I've seen peers of ours forget where they came from as their foundations crumble below them. I've talked to musicians who have never slept on a floor or ridden in a van.

Sometimes they can't even imagine sharing a tour bus with their crew members. With few exceptions, their stories all end the same.

The open road courses through our veins and breathes life into our lungs. But there is such thing as excess, indulgence, and overdose. Enrich the idle hours of those inevitably long, hurry-up-and-wait days with something that stimulates rather than numbs. Nurture the hearts and minds of the audience that let their fists turn into brave ears. Hang on tight and know when to get off.

Nagel

ENJOY SOLITUDE

Musician and writer
Muff Potter, Blood Robots
Living in Berlin, Germany
On the road: 18 years

"Don't you ever get bored being on the road all by yourself?"

This is a question I get asked almost every night on my reading tours, and I always answer the same: I am never bored when I'm alone. I'm only bored when I'm with people that are bored. When you bore each other stiff, you drag each other down with your dullness.

Boredom is a beast that hungers only for more boredom, and it is always hungry.

When alone, you can read, write, sleep, or stare out the window. Four activities that even at home I think every day should be made at least six hours longer for.

I love traveling on my own. You're more attentive. You see more, hear more, you're less distracted. Being alone is exciting! Some may call it autism. For me, it's a party.

Though at times, I have to admit that it can be quite exhausting. For example, when you've just released a new book and your agent thought it a good idea to do all the big cities one after another at the front of the tour. Added to the anxiety of performing a new program, throw in long taxi rides and interviews every day, not to forget all the e-mails and texts from your good old friends that go "Hey, buddy, can you put me on the list

tonight+10. Thanks"—preferably sent five minutes before show time—
"...oh and by the way, I made a list of five crazy spots I'm gonna take you
after the show. We're gonna get wasted!!!"

It's then that you wish for not only those extra six hours a day, but for
band mates, a tour manager, a tech, a merch man—anyone to cover for
you and just leave you in peace with your book and your handful of
painkillers.

But boring? It never is. A lot of times on these reading tours, I don't
want the train ride to end, I don't wanna be in the next city because I'm
not done with reading, writing, sleeping, or staring out the window yet.

When I'm on tour with band and crew, I hardly get any of these things
done. I'm too agitated to write, too distracted to read, I stare at the back of
the guy in front of me for hours, or I yell infantile shit through the bus
just like everybody else. Of course, that's fun. Extending your childhood
has always been a healthy part of being in a band. Only, it can get a little
old after a while.

For years, my ex-band had the same argument before every tour: van
and hotels, or nightliner?

I never wanted the nightliner. It might look cool from the outside, but
besides smelling like a dead cat in the rain after roughly half a day, causing
serious claustrophobia, and always being either too hot or too cold, these
sickness-spreading machines steal every last bit of privacy you have on a
tour.

My band mates would argue that by sleeping on the bus, we'd have
more time in the cities during the day. That's true, in theory; you do have
more time—but only where you don't need it. During the day, we'd just
end up hanging around in empty clubs on the edge of the town, apathetic,
like retarded, or maybe retired, sending each other e-mails and eating tons
of sandwiches for no other reason than ultimate boredom. And at night,
when all our old and new friends were going out to the next five crazy
spots, we'd have to leave for the next town. So instead we'd continue
drinking on the bus, and by the time we crawl into our bunks, we're prac-
tically in the next town, doomed to sleep through the afternoon we were

meant to be taking advantage of. What a waste. (You see, distances between cities in Europe are rarely far enough to be an excuse for this undignified kind of travelling).

But somehow, every time we went out, our tour manager would calculate that a nightliner was less expensive than van and hotels, and that would be the end of the discussion.

I really don't want to sound like the whining old man that I am, but so much for the glamorous myth of nightliners.

Now when I'm on a reading tour, I travel by train and taxi, and I always travel alone. I don't necessarily tell the promoters, hoping they'll expect me to come with a tour manager and book a double room. Beds in Europe are rather small, you know.

Nagel.

www.nagel2000.de

Franz Nicolay

BEING A TOURING PERFORMER IS NOT UNLIKE BEING IN THE MILITARY

Musician
World/Inferno Friendship Society, the Hold Steady, my own damn self;
in that chronological order
On the road for 12 years and counting

Being on the road for a living is an exercise in dual existence and of embodying, on demand, mutually exclusive personae. You are pauper by day and prince by night, both poor and pampered; ignored and celebrated; disciplined and Dionysian; and responsible for only two things, essentially, per day—sound check and show time (and, really, be on time for sound check)—but ultimately only responsible to yourself and your dignity; since for most of us, only we will notice if we stop living up to our own standards. In this sense it is a daily exercise in mental discipline.

I invite you to consider yourself as having signed up for the military. In point of fact there is a great deal of similarity between touring life and military life: small groups of men (and it is, almost always, still men) of disparate backgrounds, bonded by close quarters, foreign places, and meager rations; engaged in activities of dubious purpose but governed by vague and powerful ideals: patriotism, punk rock, machismo. The rules are the same: Do your job. Pack light and tight, with a day uniform and a night uniform. Defend your gang, don't get off the boat, beware of strangers. Sleep stacked three-deep in bus bunks like submariners or curled in hard foxhole-corners. Release your tensions in promiscuity, alcoholism, and violence. Keep your mouth shut. Keep your feet dry. Above all, don't complain. You will be broken down and rebuilt in ways in which you may not recognize yourself. There are lifers in both fields, but for most of your peers, their glory days will be defining, traumatic, short-lived, and remembered with a combination of nostalgia and relief.

And like army men and women, when we finish our tours of duty, even if we remain in the touring life, we lose the taste for adventure: We return, like Second World war soldiers, creating the Eisenhower suburbs and quickly domesticate. We pair off, leave the cities for places like upstate New York, Oxford, and Redding; places within driving distance of an airport and a music scene but far from chance encounters with tour acquaintances. We drink quietly and alone, avoid loud bars and rock shows as places of unwanted entertainment and possibility. We tell and retell, buff and hone, our debauched and criminal war stories with those who were there, when we see them; in a mutual, fictionalizing reassurance that what we did had some meaning, that we fought for the right side and maybe even won a small skirmish here and there. To outsiders, we no longer brag: We're no longer sure we were noble.

You don't travel for comfort; you travel to justify the daily discomfort—what in the last century they would've called existential neurosis. It's a way of therapy: the nagging doubt, sadness, weariness, the sense of being a stranger in a world viewed at an oblique angle; suddenly, miraculously, it all has a reason—you've been travelling. It's not your past, your guilt, your family. It's just the road; you *are* tired and sore, you *are* a stranger. Having solved that question, you can turn your mind to other contemplations.

Mike Park

MUSIC IS AWESOME

Plea for Peace, Asian Man Records

The excitement of being in your first band, playing your first shows, and then going on your first tour. Some of the best memories in my life. In 1989 I dropped out of college and started doing the band thing full time. Averaged 200 shows a year from 1989–1996, and then I hit a wall. I was completely exhausted. Never toured in a bus, just a fifteen-passenger van (five different vans). For the first four years, we never even stayed in a hotel. We would ask people from the stage if we could stay at someone's home. Slept in trailer parks, cat-shit-filled apartments, in the club, in rest areas, and once in awhile we'd get lucky and have a relative living in the area where we would get fed a nice meal and some bedding.

My pay was $5 a day from 1989–1992. Peak salary was in 1996 where I got $400 a week. Playing shows on consecutive nights in Reno, Salt Lake City, Denver, and then St. Louis, meant driving straight after the show with no sleep, and, over 1,800 miles later, being out of your mind from exhaustion. This was my life for seven years.

I love music very much and feel blessed to have it be a huge part of my life. But the joy of playing live has really been lost for me. Sometimes I love playing live, but sometimes I hate it. Therefore I rarely play shows. I took five years off from playing any live shows. In 2004 I tried to do it full time, but only managed about a hundred shows a year from 2004–2008, and

I've again hit that wall. I've played three shows in the last two years. I don't know why this is problem for me. I still enjoy seeing live music, and I love playing guitar for my children at home, but the whole process of getting ready to do a show is just a mental strain. I can't really explain why.

When I watch other bands, I wonder if they are just going through the motions on stage or if they are genuinely in love with what they are doing. Many times, I would just go through the motions, and I felt like a whore and promised myself I would never do that again. But alas, I do love music so very much and hope that one day my body and soul will be able to enjoy the live experience I once did as a young man.

peace, mike park

Nuno Pereira

REMEMBER WHY IT IS YOU'RE DOING WHAT YOU DO

A Wilhelm Scream
12 years on the road

$\mathbf{M}$y name is Nuno Pereira. I sing in the band A Wilhelm Scream. I also work at No Problemo taqueria in New Bedford, Massachusetts. My touring in the U.S. and abroad has spanned twelve years. This is my story.

Remember why it is you're doing what you do.

It has to be nine or ten years ago, now, me and the guys were in the middle of what was then our longest tour of our young careers. It was wintertime and we were pitifully broke, cold, sick, and hungry. I had been battling influenza for days.

As we pulled up to the venue, it was painfully obvious that no one was there, or going to be there, and we were sunk. This venue in particular was also a squat/apartments for a few of the staff we recalled after too many frozen minutes. So we proceeded to ring a few bells. After waiting a bit, a gentleman emerged, half asleep. We explained who we were and that we were there to play a gig we'd booked months ago. The dude was baffled.

While we were pleading our case, four or five kids had shown up. They too were there for the show. They were the only kids to show up that cold night.

I lost it. I stormed back to the van to cough and sulk. I told the rest of the guys we should just leave and head to the next, hopefully warmer, tour stop. They knew I was sick. I tried to milk it. Then it happened.

The van door opened and my friend Trevor jumped in. He looked at me and proceeded to drop a heap of knowledge on me. He started out by saying he knew I was sick and that we all were upset about the venues mistake, but they were willing to let us play anyway. He told me that those four kids that showed up to see us would remember this night for a long time—the night one of their favorite bands could have split but instead put on a private show just for them.

He was right. I felt ashamed for thinking I was bigger than the whole. I also felt a little bit of life and warmth come back to me.

We played our hearts out for those guys and for each other. I learned that night that I will never be more important than the music or the dynamic between artist and fan. Never lose sight of that, and the fans you make will always support you. Come hell or high water.

The Rev. Peyton

YOU DON'T KNOW AS MUCH AS YOU THINK YOU KNOW

The Rev. Peyton's Big Damn Band

All of my heroes were road warriors, travelers, vagabonds, highway poets, musicians that had seen the world. I longed to be among that number. We were good when we set out on the road. We had tons of potential, but the road made us great. I am very grateful for that. I set out on the road to play music. It changed me. I'm the better for it, but the solace that comes with naivety used to be comforting. However, I didn't know it then. You don't know as much as you think you know.

In almost a decade on the road, I have spent time and befriended NBA stars, famous actors, famous musicians, and some of the most well-known and richest people in the world. The same can be said of bums, hobos, artists, weirdoes, freaks, and so many great folks in between. I have dined at castles in France; I have been broke and heating up ramen noodles with the hot water from the gas-station coffee maker. I have been invited into so many people's homes for a home-cooked meal, and I have been run off of property for trying to get some sleep in our van. There have been times when I was broke, and I know I have been given someone's last dollar. I have been robbed of all my possessions in a foreign country, standing on the street, feeling about as far from home as you can feel.

I have watched the road devour people. Drugs, alcohol, time spent away from family and friends. It can destroy people. Everyone that lasts out here realizes that about the substance abuse. It will destroy you in the end. The other side of the coin is that the road has made people. It destroys, and then it turns around and makes someone. It is different out here than most people think. I have watched people have panic attacks from road stress. I have seen people beg for tickets home. A friend of mine who was a train hobo said our life was all the stress and hardship of a train hobo, only with a crazy tight schedule to keep. He loves the road, but not necessarily touring. I am addicted to the road and the tour.

The sun setting over mountains and rising over oceans never gets old. The Grand Canyon never gets old. The Redwood forest never gets old. The songs and the fans and the love never get old. Walking into a rest area and watching some creep jerking off right at the urinal does get old. Thieves, crooks, hustlers, predators of all types get old.

The truth is . . . I have seen the best of people. I have seen some of the worst of people. There is so much beauty in the world. Most people are asleep to it. There is so much more out there than most people could ever imagine. There are a lot of different ways of doing things. Life can be hard, the road can be hard, and people have to survive. You have to adapt. If you have a heart, you have to extend a hand every now and then. If it doesn't change you, then you are not awake. You don't know as much as you think you know. Period.

Michael Semrad

THE MUSE THAT CHASES . . .

Haywood Yards
10 years on the road

I am inspired by my blood, my heritage, and the yellow lines that chase each other down the highways. At times, I am hit with blasts of inspiration. It could be from the color of the fields in Nebraska and the working man's grin, or the smell of the lake in Chicago and the mountains in Colorado. On the road, or wherever it happens, I force myself to write these "free" blasts of inspirations down. I am obsessive at times. I understand and respect this behavior within myself. But in the end, rather than forgetting a great idea, I encapsulate it and let it reside. My uncle toured in the late '50s, out of Omaha, with the Grand Ole' Opry's first "Road Show," featuring the likes of Johnny Cash, Minnie Pearl, Little Jimmy Dickens, and George Jones, to name a few. He would tell me of the late-night whiskey-soaked card games filled with smoke, for which the players would sometimes gamble their homes, cars, and guitars away. Sometimes these things would spur the idea for a song as they lay half asleep on a whirling steel beast, floating down the highways. Anything, he said, was fodder for a song idea. Now, I am not saying to gamble away your home and your belongings to become inspired (but if that's what it takes, then let it ride). But I am suggesting to be ALERT and DON'T let these ideas float by the wayside, spin into the black, and be gone forever. And no matter where I am, I seize that moment and encapsulate that thought, whether fruitful or not, as if you're planting a seed to give it a chance to grow. At least I know it's mine, once it's down. It won't escape. It's yours, now . . . forever.

James Smith

The Drowning Men
Years touring: 2

You quickly become closer to your closest friends when you accidentally consume their puke and urine while spending most of the day in a stinky van. The challenges of the road can make a good band great, a great band break up, or a group of people fully realize this is what they wanted to do their entire lives. This story is about a band finding their tour legs.

In early 2011, Flogging Molly invited us on the road for six weeks. Going into this tour, we had heard legends of their fans being very hard on the openers. We had basically been a bar band, done some regional tours, and now we were playing to larger numbers than we were used to, every night. Playing with a band that you haven't established a relationship with, the last thing you want to do is make their night more difficult. So we showed up on time, worked hard, and stayed out of the band's and crew's way. Being the opener, just appreciate what's given to you and don't demand anything.

They quickly saw this wasn't a vacation for us, but a job. A job we wanted and treated as such. They took a liking to us and gave us advice and help. Their guitar tech, Badger, said, "Y'all need to get your stage performance together so you can quit your day jobs. Better yet, y'all need to invent something and quit this band shit altogether." Chris, the monitor engineer, typically sleeps during the opener's sound check and set. But most nights he would help us with our monitor mix and sometimes actually do monitors for us. Some nights, Badger would tech when we had problems during our set. All in all, these people took valuable time out of their lives and helped us, even though they didn't have to, and we are forever thankful.

When someone gives you advice, or "road wisdom," don't brush it off. They didn't have to share this with you, and you could have learned it the hard way.

But as far as a single rule of thumb, the best approach to surviving on the road is to do your job and be invisible.

Jon Snodgrass

TRY THE THING AT THE PLACE, EAT, & SLEEP

19 years of touring. If this book comes out in 2012, that's half my life.

If you're going to new places you've never been, you need to *try* and experience something new every day. It's hard, though, 'cuz you're in a constant rush and even neglecting to do things like eat or sleep.

Ask someone where the best place to eat is. The good place, the mom & pop place. The place they are proud to say is in their town. Where they would eat, I guess. When you get there, you need to order "the Thing"— it's the thing they are known for at "the Place."

It might be waffles & sausage gravy in Bremerton, Washington; pizza with tuna fish & onions in Germany; proper BBQ when down south; legit tacos even further south; or what goulash actually is while visiting Hungary. I was wrong about goulash, and many other things. It's good to learn stuff. Talk to folks and get informed. If you actually end up going to Bremerton, take the boat from Seattle.

The show may very well be at "the Place" with "the Thing."

For example: If you've never been to the Triple Rock Social Club in Minneapolis, you really gotta get out there. Try and go to the beach anytime it's possible. Even if it's just to take a shower or see if there's a hammock down there. We're lucky, ya know? People spend a lot of money on these types of vacations. Years ago on a Drag the River tour, we went to Niagara Falls. I feel fortunate to get to do what I do. Anyhow, I never actually saw the falls that time. I did get a great & very much needed nap. We parked real close, and it sounded like a giant white-noise machine. The sun was going down, the windows came down, the wind was perfect. Best nap ever.

So, remember to eat and sleep, and do it right while you're at it. And drink a lot of water . . . and super-hot, no-sugar-added pineapple juice, if you lose your voice.

And be considerate, 'cuz we're all in it together.

Tobe

FREE WILL AND MY OPEN MIND

When asked what is the most important thing I carry on the road with me, that's what comes to mind first. I mean, sure there's lots of literal things like guitars, certain books, weird belongings hatched out of superstitions, and other nonsense—but my open mind and sense of adventure is what I cherish the most and is my engine propelling me down this endless road of lunacy. A wise man once told me, "Don't be that one old motherfucker on the porch with no story to tell!" To this day, I've never forgotten that. I'm a lucky son of a bitch that gets to travel the world with my buddies in the name of punk rock, but the experiences are what makes it worth it. Not to mention THIS SHIT WILL NOT LAST FOREVER. By just going with where life takes me, I've been able to see things that most will never see in an entire lifetime. Whether it's eating bizarre foods, drinking exorbitant amounts of different liquors, taking solo walkabouts in foreign lands, or just striking up conversations with complete strangers, my story wouldn't be written without my sometimes-dangerous open-mindedness. I've spent time with the lowest of the low, rubbed elbows with the trappings of the American power structure, seen sights that most won't, seen musical performances of legend, and met the most colorful of folk. I've experienced romance, heartbreak, and the beauty of spontaneity. When life presents a path to travel down, you charge down it blindly, with arms wide open. Sure, my free will and open mind get me in trouble more often than not, but I guarantee I will not be that one old motherfucker on the porch with no story to tell.

Scott Toepfer

ENJOY THE SIMPLE

Photographer
On the road 10 years

It would be a misstep to consider myself anything but a "kid" in this scheme of things. I've been taking photographs for a while and trying desperately every day to stay moving in any sort of way. I've changed my residence at least once a year, every year, since I was seventeen years old, and it's been a quite a ride since.

I began traveling with some sort of conscious plan midway through college. I would consider most of the time before then as unsorted, postadolescent wanderings without any sort of purpose but to take photographs. Making the decision to have a purpose, to explore with the camera and live through it, is probably the most forward and formative decision I've made.

Being the photographer has taught me about becoming intimate with otherwise total strangers, and while some become friends on the road, others do not. The key as I've seen it is to simply enjoy people as they are, for who they are. These people, like you, are on the road, and you might not cross paths with them again for years, if ever. So enjoy the time you have with a smile, share the ground you stand on, and let common ground create rather than divide.

When it comes to the road, it's always been about "simple." If there is anything someone could take away from my own wanderings, it would be the value of keeping things simple. We are resilient beings, capable of adapting in crisis. When you leave certain things behind, or don't plan a trip to the I's and T's, all for the sake of adventure and living by some level of spontaneity, you risk little more than an uncomfortable night's sleep (or two). Keeping your wits about you and using common sense is all that most people need. Conversely, by over-planning or micromanaging the road, you paralyze it in a way that keeps you from truly experiencing the culture that surrounds the path. The goal is to be a traveler, not a tourist. So keep it simple, enjoy the ride, and use common sense.

The troubadours are a dying breed, and a culture to be cherished. The comfort of home is a bit of a mystery that I am only now beginning to understand. And while I am constantly collecting visual memories to put in permanent places . . . I continue to yearn for the calm and uncertainty that a little trip to anywhere can bring.

Mitchell Townsend

SOME PEOPLE ARE ACTUALLY COOLER THAN YOU. ACT ACCORDINGLY.

On the road 16 years

I started dragging my ass out into the wild beer yonder back in 1995, and one of the first things that made an impression on me was the variety of different people that you meet on a day-to-day basis who are all doing their own little part in making the show go on. Door guys, stagehands, production assistants, catering folks, runners, the dudes in the bathroom with the candy bowl who hand you the little towel, and so on. All of these people, no matter what their job title is, are there for the same reason you are: to try to make a few dimes and help the show go off without a hitch, so that hopefully they can clock in again the next day and make a few more dimes. With the exception of the inevitable bad eggs you will encounter here and there, these are good people and they deserve your respect.

It has always blown my mind how many people get out on tour and think they have suddenly earned the right to act like entitled, self-obsessed, disrespectful assholes, particularly towards the people in the building that are actually doing some real work, as opposed to just sitting in a dressing room all day whining that the wi-fi signal isn't strong enough for you to go on FaceBook and look at photos of yourself. The fact that you play music, or work for someone who is playing music, doesn't make you special. Brain surgeons are special. Astronauts are special. What can you do? Play the bass line to every song on the first Cure record? So can my niece, and she's twelve.

I have seen Liam Gallagher walk into a different arena every day and shake hands with door guys and ask them their names. I have seen Dave Grohl ask the guy clearing the plates off the tables in catering if he wants to do a shot of Crown with him. Those guys' bands play soccer stadiums. Your band does not. If those guys aren't dicks, then you can pull off not being one, too. Whether you are the next Justin Bieber or the bass tech for a Frankie Goes to Hollywood Tribute band, you are walking into someone else's world every day, and you are actually the one who is lucky to be there. You are not gracing everyone out there with your presence.

However, if you treat people with respect and sincerity, they will likely end up feeling like you actually are. You want people to talk about your band? Be cool to them. They will spend the next year telling everyone who comes through their venue, "Dude, I can't wait until Jousting the Dark Dragon of Twilight's Dividing Ashes comes back to town! Those guys are cool as shit." Trust me, that is way more helpful to your cause than them saying, "Those assholes were jerks to everyone and threw a fit because the shower curtain in the dressing room wasn't vegan. Fuck those guys."

Be cool to people, and you will end up making friends out on the road that you will have for the rest of your life—and that is the best thing you will get out of being out there in the first place. The skull-crushing hangovers and the severe sleep deprivation are mere added bonuses. I wish you nothing but the best of luck. Have fun out there.

Frank Turner

LEAVE THINGS AS YOU FIND THEM

On the road 13 years

I've been touring for a long time, and a fair amount of that time was on my own—I spent years traveling around the U.K. on the train with a rucksack and a guitar, doing stage shout-outs for places to stay. I'd go for days, weeks, even, without seeing anyone I'd ever met before. Obviously that experience taught me a lot about self-reliance, about being decisive, about making friends. But I guess one of the most important things I've realized is that it's best to leave the world as you found it when you arrived.

A lot of young people I see in bands going out on their first tours will get into the bullshit rock 'n' roll clichés. They'll trash dressing rooms, tag the walls with marker pens, that kind of thing. They'll get super-drunk and start hitting on the promoter's girlfriend or something like that, taking advantage of the old adage that "What goes on tour stays on tour," or some such nonsense. They'll be in a different town the next day and can leave wreckage in their wake, and if they're ever challenged on the subject they'll make some crass, flippant remark about Mötley Crüe.

But here's the truth of it—if you want to live on the road for longer than some drunken teenage gap year, you'll encounter all these people again. They'll spread the word about you being an arsehole, and the world will start turning its back on you, and rightly so. Most people understand that they should act respectfully to those around them in normal life; if touring is what you want for your normal life, the same rules apply.

An existence on the road is one in which you depend on the kindness of strangers more than you do in normal, civilian life. So treat the people around you with politeness and respect, help the guys at the venue load out at the end of the night (or at least get out of their way), make your bed and wash up your dishes for the people who put you up, share your rider, and be considerate. Remember that you're just an itinerant entertainer, which isn't much to shout about in the grand scheme of things, and someone just like you will be doing it all again in the same place the next night. You make your own luck on the road, so be all these things, leave the world as you find it, and the road will treat you well.

"YOU MAKE YOUR OWN
LUCK ON THE ROAD...
LEAVE THE WORLD AS
YOU FIND IT, AND THE
ROAD WILL TREAT
YOU WELL."

Frank Turner

Tim Vantol

LET THEM BEG YOU TO COME BACK

On the road 8 years

There is nothing as cool as traveling the world and play your songs in front of a bunch of people. Seeing things that you probably wouldn't see if you didn't tour as a musician, meeting lots of great people, and learning more than any school can teach you. That's the great part of touring.

There is one thing i learned before i started to go on tour when i helped out at a small local venue: Be thankful towards all the people who are helping you out, even if things are not going exactly like planned. Most of the people will try their best to set up a show where the kids can have a good time and where you can play your songs. It doesn't make any sense to walk around and being pissed off 'cause one (out of six) monitors is broken— nothing to do about that.

Not in a good mood? That can always happen, but walking around being grumpy is not gonna make it any better. You are there to play the best show ever and to have lots of fun, get your ass on the stage, enjoy, and let them beg you to come back for another show. Being a dick on stage can actually take away your touring dream. 'Cause the internet will give you a hand spreading the word of you being disrespectful and ungrateful.

These days, it's not only about how great you are as a musician or band; in my opinion, every idiot can go on tour. It's all about respect, being thankful, and helping each other out—only those will survive to burn more and more miles.

Greg Walker

VIEWS FROM THE DRIVER'S SIDE

Tour bus driver
6 years out on the road

We, as drivers, get paid to sleep. Not a bad gig, if you can get it. But it's true. A job like this could be deadly without proper rest and sleep. Yes, we also get paid to drive the band and crew from city to city with safety being the number one goal. We are also responsible for keeping the bus running and getting any mechanical problems resolved without any disruption to the tour.

Although it may sound like an easy job, it can be very stressful at times. Sleeping at different times every day, waking up at odd hours, and driving hundreds of miles through the night in all types of weather takes a responsible and professional driver. If you're on a bus for the first time and you find you don't have a responsible driver, call your bus company and have him or her replaced.

Take care of your bus. You are paying for the bus during your tour, but that doesn't mean you can destroy it unless you're willing to pay for the damages. Get wasted and start breaking things, and you'll find things won't get fixed. Why fix something when it will just happen again. Treat the bus like your home, which it is, and you'll be fine.

Keep it clean. You'll be in a confined area with little privacy except your own personal bunk. It's important to respect the common areas of the bus, which can get very messy at times. While we as drivers will take out the trash, wipe down counters, sweep or vacuum the front lounge area, that doesn't mean we are on the bus all the time. If the trash is overflowing before we get back, empty it. The trash can is in the same place every day, and we don't move it from one place to another. If you leave empty beer bottles, cups, empty pizza boxes, or used Kleenex on the counters or tables, we assume you have left them there for a reason and can you expect to find them in the same place when you wake up.

If you can afford a bus for your tour, you're doing better financially than 90 percent of the bands out there. And you'll be on the road doing what you love to do. If you don't love it, don't do it.

I love what I do, and I'm fortunate and honored to drive the bands I work for. I travel the roads of the United States and Canada and visit cities big and small. But what stands out above all else is the camaraderie that develops during a tour with everyone on the bus. It's an amazing experience with every tour, and equally amazing for me to get to know each member of the band and crew, and even their families, too. While it's great to be able to make a living and pay the bills on the road, I have noticed over the years and working with different groups, money is not always the motivating reason for being on the road. It's the love of writing the music, performing in front of crowds whether large or small, and the friendships that develop for years to come. Many bands will never get this experience.

So be nice and respectful to each other, be nice and respectful to the crews at the various venues you'll be going to, and be nice and respectful to your driver. After all, we have your lives in our hands, every day.

More importantly, be nice to your fans . . . they are the ones paying to see you!

Nathan Walker

Drummer
Bands I've played/teched for: Lit, Kerli, Lucy Walsh, the Strays, the
Cornfed Project, Rufio, Die Trying, Zebrahead, Sugar Ray, Sublime w/
Rome
9-plus years on the road

I started touring at the age of nineteen as a drum tech. As most touring people do, my first tours were in a van. I learned quickly the etiquette of touring in a van with people you don't really know. You don't get any personal space at all, and you have to learn to adapt quick in small areas with a bunch of people and random belongings all over the place. The long days and hardly any sleeping can get to you quick. My first couple tours, I started as a drum tech then moved into a tour manager position, sleep was hard to come by. With only a few hours a night at a hotel, the only sleep I ever got was on the floor between seats. Not a glamorous way to be on the road. But I eventually got used to it, even though those first couple tours were rough. Definitely learn to respect all the people around you and their personal space, if you could ever find any. There were times I would want to hop on a plane and go home, and there were times I never wanted to leave the family of friends I made being hired to travel with them.

Those tours in the beginning and learning the ropes and figuring out how to deal with crazy-ass people have helped me understand what it really takes to live a life on the road. Everyone has his or her own mindset of what it means to tour and what to make of it. For me, it's always been a job, whether it's playing drums or teching; I've always tried to look at it in a professional way, that I'm getting paid to do this. I wouldn't go to a normal desk job or McDonald's drinking, or whatever else might happen out there. We've probably all slipped a bit, but I definitely do my absolute best in being professional and treating the road like any other job out there.

Since my first touring experience, I've been able to travel the world. I've met a lot of people and made some incredible friends. Just like it is a family out there, everyone looks out for each other, in the sense of people helping people find gigs, watching people's backs. It's a huge community out there and everyone is linked up somehow. I recommend learning how to respect everyone, no matter what your opinions or views are. Everyone is different and being on the road stuck with the same people day in and day out could get stressful. If you can respect the people that you live with in a van or bus, then touring will be a piece of cake.

Of the nine-plus years of traveling the world, endless plane flights, long days in a van and bus, the ups and downs, arguments that occur, drunken nights (and days), they have been the best times ever. I do have a great respect for being home and enjoying what I have in Orange County, but every time there is a tour or show, I cannot wait to either get to the airport or hop into a bus. Being able to make a living touring and doing what I love is the best feeling ever. It takes a lot of hard work to get there, and even harder work to deal with life on the road. Make the best of it, respect everyone, and take into consideration the type of people you choose to live with on the road.

Jim Ward

HUMILITY

At the Drive-In, Sparta, Sleepercar
On the road 17 years

My guess is that a few people will touch on this subject, seeing that it is an intertwined group of pretty solid folks who are writing in this collection, but the greatest lesson I have learned on all these years is humility. In all these years, I have seen the ups and downs of touring. I have sold records, sold out shows, traveled well, made money, lost money, quit tours, been dropped from labels, left tours out of pure exhaustion, played to no one, and all of those experiences are what make me the person I am today. I wouldn't change a thing.

I started ATDI when I was young and not very worldly. I am definitely guilty of thinking I was cooler than I was and acting the fool. It took a couple of hard knocks and a lot of educating from my band mates before I started seeing things in the right way. I am grateful every time I hit the road. I am grateful that I get to do this, that I get to go out and see the world and play music and make friends that last, who will be my friends for the rest of my life.

It is easy to feel entitled when your career is taking off and people are throwing things your way, and it is easy to feel beat up when the tide turns. If you approach the road with humility and respect, then you can handle the ups and downs.

I can sit in with almost any group of people and trade stories and laughs because of the road, because it taught me to survive by appreciating the people around me instead of worrying whether the people around me were appreciating me. I am honored to be included in the list of folks asked to say a few words about the road. It is a hell of a gang to be a part of.

William Elliott Whitmore

WATCH OUT FOR COPS

Vagabond/Storyteller/Singer
11 years on the road

If you've been on the road long enough, chances are you've had run-ins with the local Johnny Law. Whether it's Houston, Texas, or London, England, the authorities are dying to make your life hell. Some of them actually want to help, but this seems rare, and most of the troopers and deputies are out to fill their quotas. When they see a van covered in stickers pulling a trailer with out-of-state license plates, it's like blood to a shark. They're convinced that every band is full of boozed-up hoodlums ready to rob and pillage their town. Now, I may be boozed up, but I'm no hoodlum. I just want to play a show and have some fun. A good rule of thumb is get a sober driver for after the show. Seems like common sense, but 2:00 a.m. is when the sharks are out to put you in a cage. Having to spend the band fund on bailing out the guitar player can put a dent in your touring plans. Remember, the whole point to touring is to share your music with the world and put on a great show.

They're out during the daytime, too, these blood thirsty police. I was on tour with Tim Barry years ago, and he got pulled over in Texas for no apparent reason. The cop gave him and his crew a hard time about whether or not they were really traveling musicians, or drug smugglers, or terrorists planning to bomb the White House. The cop actually made them perform a song right there by the side of the highway! How humiliating and demeaning to be treated that way. No one deserves that, let alone Tim. I've had so many experiences like this that every time I see a police car my heart rate goes up. Damn them for making me feel like that. I guess my point is to be careful and stay out of the cage. You can't share music with people in a god damned cage. Also, don't carry any more weed than you can eat at one time.

Safe travels!

Jason Yawn

Beasts of No Nation, Trial by Fire
7 years on, 8 gone

The last 8 years I've spent finding my way back to a life in music through a pretty fucked up series of personal injury and strife. The only way I got through this whole period without folding in on myself or losing my mind was to create music that I hoped to someday hear echoing off cement block walls, in front of a handful of friends.

I had felt that feeling before. I knew what that was like. I wanted it again, and this period taught me just how much. All the moments I had spent in barely heated vans, holding my piss for a hundred miles until the next desert gas station, they came back to me in a new way. The memories were humbling, not romantic, as they all seemed at the time. The clarity this pain provided made me understand they represented a life that animated my being. It wasn't all a frenzied collage of rote load-ins and grind. It wasn't some fleeting phase of youthful experience marked by laughs and good times. It was a day-to-day expression of what connected me to myself, my passions, and what is truly important about life. And not a goddamn bit of it sucked.

If we played for no money and had no place to stay, someone always offered $20 bucks for gas and a floor to sleep on. When shit went bad, we always had allies in the other bands who could empathize only too well with being robbed or breaking down. Whether we played to 200 kids packed into a damp basement and singing along or to 20 blank stares on the other side of a barricade, we played for our tour mates, for ourselves, and for that feeling in our chests.

I'm not sure I could make an argument for beauty in the doldrums of touring without having lost that direct experiential connection to the road. It gave scale to the true joy of sharing music that I somehow pulled out of my head and shared with people who become friends in the process. It makes me realize how rare, fucked up, and uniquely amazing it really is to what we do. What I get to do again.

It all means everything.